For the Love of an Airplane

From Junk to Show: How Jerry Stadtmiller
Built a Lifelong Business Restoring
Antique Aircraft

Lisa Turner

Turner Creek Publishing
Hayesville NC

Whether you're an airplane nut or not, you will enjoy this wonderful true story of a man who overcomes adversity to build a business around restoring vintage aircraft. This book will draw you in with heartwarming tales and great business advice. Turner's writing is fun, tight, and inspiring.

October 21, 2024, San Diego, CA

—**Brian Tracy**, CEO of Brian Tracy International, has consulted for more than 1,000 companies, presented to more than 5 million people in more than 80 countries, and written more than 80 books.

Read Lisa's other books on Amazon and listen on Audible.
DreamTakeFlight.com

Copyright © 2024 by **Lisa Turner**

All rights reserved. This book or parts thereof may not be reproduced in any form, stored in any retrieval system, or transmitted in any form by any means—electronic, mechanical, photocopy, recording, or otherwise—without prior written permission of the publisher, except as provided by United States of America copyright law. For permission requests, write to the publisher, Turner Creek.

Lisa Turner/Turner Creek Publishing
515 Barlow Fields Drive
Hayesville/NC 28904
www.lisaturnerbooks.com

This book is a creative biography. It is written through the lens of interviews and stories as told by Jerry Stadtmiller to Lisa Turner from 2004 to 2024. Lisa also interviewed both of Jerry's sisters. Some of the names, characters, places, and events are reconstructed based on recollection and are not intended to be exact with respect to history or genealogy. Some names have been changed to protect the privacy of individuals.

The book is designed to provide inspiration as well as entertainment to readers. It is sold with the understanding that I am not trying to render psychological, legal, or any other kind of professional or business advice to the reader.

Enjoy.

For the Love of an Airplane/Lisa Turner. - 1st ed.
ISBN 978-1-7366328-4-0 Paperback
ISBN 978-1-7366328-5-7 e-Book
ISBN 978-1-7366328-6-4 Hardcover
ISBN 978-1-7366328-7-1 Audiobook

For more information on BIPE INC., go to: RestoreYourAirplane.com

To Jerry

"We make a living by what we get, but we make a life by what we give."

~Winston Churchill

Stearman – Jerry's first restoration

Contents

Foreword xiii

Preface xvii

Part One: The Early Years xix

June 3, 1936 1

1943: School 7

DC-3s 13

1945: The Frigate 19

1952: Baseball 27

Engines 33

Line Boy 39

First Flight 45

1953: The Accident 49

1954: The Cub 55

Dad 61

1955: The Fire 67

Mustang P-51 71

Sky King 75

Five Wacos 79

Florida 87

1958: Banners 89

1959: Interruptions 95

Butternut Squash 99

The Lure of a Business 103

The Birth of BIPE 107

1999: A Chance Meeting 111

2008: Andrews, North Carolina 119

Part Two: Medical Mysteries 127

A Longer Term of Service 129

The Alien 133

Incidental Findings 139

More Lives than a Cat 143

Part Three: The Stadtmiller Guide to Business 147

Vision for BIPE 151

Practicalities 156

Ethics 161

Time Management 165

Customers 169

Employees 175

Trivia 181

Lessons 187

Customer Advice 193

No Regrets.. 197

End Notes 207

"There's an airplane in here somewhere."

Foreword

Mark Twain once said, "Find a job you love, and you will never have to work a day in your life." Finding that passion is something that eludes many, having the God-given talent and the perseverance to sustain that passion for a lifetime is rare air indeed. Jerry has done both and makes it look easy and fun while reaching a level of excellence that is hard to put into words, and even pictures don't do it justice.

I was a young flight instructor at the Institute of Aviation at the University of Illinois when I first crossed paths with Jerry at the Annual National Stearman Fly-in, in Galesburg, Illinois. I was fortunate to fly the Institute's Stearman to the fly-in. Jerry was hosting various clinics, and a few of his restorations were there. I listened at a distance to his humble advice on restoration techniques for aspiring Stearman restorers.

Jerry was awarded the coveted Charles Taylor Award from the FAA in 2005. The mechanic Charles Taylor worked for the Wright Brothers. The Charles Taylor Award is given by the FAA to select aviation mechanics who have worked in aviation for at least 50 years and meet standards of excellence in work and in character. Jerry emulates the standards that other craftspeople aspire to.

After the clinic ended, Jerry was surrounded by Stearman Groupies, wanting more of his incredible knowledge and endless humble humor. As I tried to get closer to him, it was like trying to get close to the Pope after Christmas mass. If only, I thought, I could fly a Stearman he restored ... if only I could afford to own a Stearman restored by Jerry ... it was quite a nice dream for an 18-year-old college student.

I finally got the nerve to make my way through the crowd. "Jerry, do you have time for a question?" I asked.

Jerry gave me his full attention. "Well, that depends; is it an easy one or a difficult one?"

"Easy, I think. Why?"

"Well, the simple questions are five dollars, the difficult ones are double or triple that, especially if I have to look it up," replied Jerry, with a smile. The crowd around him laughed.

After our meeting, I continued to dream about a Stearman and finally got the courage to call Jerry some thirty years later.

"We're not getting any younger, you know; do you really want a Stearman? Let's find you a project to restore," said Jerry.

You must understand that Jerry's definition of "project" is not what most folks would envision as a project. This "project" Jerry found had been piled in the back of someone's hangar in Florida for fifty-seven years. Jerry sent me pictures asking me if I wanted to proceed.

"Why would you haul this all the way to North Carolina when you could just take it to the local dump?" I asked.

Jerry being Jerry said, "Because it's a Stearman."

Twenty-four months later, I was flying the most beautiful Stearman I've ever been in.

With every passing day, we are losing the knowledge and talent of the likes of Jerry. Throughout my fifty-plus years in aviation, I have been blessed to shake the hands of some of my heroes ... Bob Hoover, Neil Armstrong, Fred Haise, Bill Anders, to mention a few. But Jerry tops my list for not only his passion, but for the humble kindness he has brought to so many.

Lisa tells the story as no one else can.

All for the love of an airplane.

—Gary Allen, NWA/DAL Retired Captain, Lake Stevens, Washington, United States.

October 20, 2024

Preface

I kept waiting for the other shoe to drop.

As humans, we all have persevered through catastrophe. Difficulties and adversity help define us. Our character is shaped by the hands of genetics, culture, and luck.

The day I met Jerry in 1999, he displayed a delightful combination of confidence, grace, and humor. You wouldn't know that he'd experienced as many survival moments as a cat on its ninth encounter. A student in his fabric covering class, I couldn't help but be intrigued by the man.

When I discovered a life story full of adversity and more luck that any human is entitled to, I was drawn in and we became fast friends. I had to find out more about Jerry Stadtmiller.

Come with me on this flight.

Part One:
The Early Years

"Do not fear the winds of adversity. Remember, a kite rises against the wind rather than with it."
~Winston Churchill

Chapter 1

June 3, 1936

"I'm going into labor," said Martha.

"You're not far enough along, Mom," said Bea.

"I can't help it."

"Of course you can't." Seventeen-year-old Bea turned to her younger sister Arline. "We will find Dr. Cook."

"Please, yes," voiced Martha, sitting down at the edge of the bed with a groan. She held her swollen belly and rocked back and forth.

Bea and Arline left the small bedroom and went downstairs to the kitchen. Arline shook her head vigorously on the way down the narrow staircase. "The baby is months early!"

"I know. It is not likely to survive. Don't say that to Mom."

"She knows."

For the Love of an Airplane

The sisters went into the kitchen. Arline sat down at the round table next to the wood stove while Bea pulled out a small wash tub with towels from the closet.

"Arline, go down the street please to the Thomas's who have a telephone, and ask the operator to get Dr. Cook. He may not get here in time, so when you get back, we will help Mom."

Arline nodded. "What about Dad?"

"I don't want to run down to the shop now. Mom needs us here. He'll be home later. There's nothing he can do."

"Did Glenn leave with Bill for the islands yet?"

"He did," said Bea. "It's just as well. I'd rather not explain to them they have a baby brother ... maybe."

Two hours later, Martha went into labor. Bea and Arline were at her side when Dr. Cook arrived, along with Martha's husband, Andy. Bea and Dr. Cook helped Martha, and Andy and Arline moved outside the room.

Andy shook his head. "The baby is too early."

"I know," said Arline. "We will do what we can."

They heard gurgling noises and a shout.

"It's a boy."

A short time later, Dr. Cook came out with a somber, studied expression. He motioned for the girls to follow him downstairs.

"Please prepare yourselves. The child's birth weight is two pounds five ounces. He is unlikely to live. I'm going to get you some Dextri-Maltose to add to evaporated milk for him. You'll need an eye-dropper and a warm place; probably right here in the kitchen near the stove."

He put his stethoscope and instruments back in his case. No one said a word. The stillness reminded Arline of the winter nights after a snow. It was as if a blanket covered their thoughts.

Andy came down into the kitchen. "They're resting." He took a deep breath and exhaled. "It's not looking promising. The baby isn't making a sound."

"The baby is over three months early," said Dr. Cook in a whisper. "In my experience, I've never seen a baby this premature make it. There just isn't enough development in the body systems internally to survive. Let's hope for the best. Perhaps we'll be fortunate. Pray."

Arline squeezed her eyes shut. A tear escaped and ran down her cheek.

Dr. Cook returned an hour later with formula and eyedroppers. They located the baby in the kitchen near the stove in a shoebox lined with a clean white cotton t-shirt.

Dr. Cook turned to Bea. "His lungs aren't fully developed; he will make noises but can't cry yet. He may not be able to drink anything. The internal organs may not be far enough along for any digestion. But you can try with the dropper and a little warm formula. I'll return in the morning to check on Martha."

Dr. Cook looked into the shoebox one more time. He turned to the two sisters. "Don't get attached to the baby."

That night Bea and Arline took turns watching over the tiny baby boy. They talked and fussed over him, and Bea held him as you would a small bird in the palm of her hand for feeding. He drank bits of the milk and then spit it up. They persevered.

"It's too bad Mom can't breastfeed," said Arline.

"She's not producing. I can't believe how early this baby is."

The sisters looked at each other in amazement. "Over 12 weeks," said Bea.

Early the next morning Bea was startled at a loud knock on the front door. The sisters had taken turns napping on the old wood bench next to the stove, although neither one of them could sleep.

"That must be Dr. Cook," said Arline, getting up and going to the door.

Dr. Cook came into the kitchen and hesitated, trying to get a read on the sisters' faces. Then he looked into the shoebox. "My word, he survived the night."

Bea smiled. "He's tough. He's been sleeping but spits up the formula."

Dr. Cook displayed a guarded smile. "This is good news. He's probably not able to digest anything yet. Chances are still very slim that he will make it. All of his organs are developing, so it will be a miracle indeed if he lives through the next few days. Keep doing what you're doing. Be sure to sterilize the glass droppers. Babies this small can develop infections and a host of ailments."

Bea looked into the shoebox. The small baby opened and closed his eyes, and one tiny hand swept across his forehead, jerkily, as if to remove a cobweb. He looked up and tried to move his head in a tiny tremor. Then he closed his eyes. The eyelashes were as small as grains of sand. The baby's length was about eight inches; the feet were the size of Bea's thumb.

Bea placed her index finger gently on the top of the baby's head and stroked a few times. "Gerald Carl Stadtmiller. That's a pretty big name for a miniature thing like you."

"Jerry. We will call him Jerry," piped up Arline.

The sisters looked at each other and smiled.

"Don't be afraid to take a big step. You can't cross a chasm in two small jumps."
~David Lloyd George

Chapter 2

1943: School

The dreaded day had arrived.

"Come along, Jerry. I'll walk with you to your first day of school." His mother reached out for Jerry's hand.

Jerry knew he had to go. There was no escaping it. Could he feign illness? Probably not.

As his mother walked him the five blocks to Holy Family Catholic School, he could feel the fear building in his chest.

"Do you want me to meet you here at this spot after school?" Martha kneeled in front of Jerry and straightened his shirt collar.

For the Love of an Airplane

"No, I can walk home okay."

"Do what the nuns tell you, Jerry."

"Yes, Mom, yes."

He watched his mother turn around and start back up the block.

I can turn around right now and no one will know. I can go hide.

The stone edifice towered in front of him, dwarfing the surrounding buildings. He had passed this school many times with his family as they drove about town. Now he was here all by himself. A little over thirty-eight pounds, his four-foot frame was slim and lean. His brown hair was closely cropped. He clutched a small paper lunch bag.

Jerry took a few steps toward the building, still feeling drawn back to home, conflicted about what to do. He was frightened by a noise behind him. He turned to see a nun reaching for him.

"Welcome! This way. We'll get you started with your classmates," she said, gripping Jerry's shoulders as if she knew exactly what he was thinking.

So much for the idea of turning around.

Once inside, Jerry was lined up with a group of boys as the administrators took names and assigned classrooms. Nuns in crisp contrast uniforms bustled about; the noise levels began to lower as everything was organized. There was little to do except follow his classmates. *Trapped.*

"Why are they separating the boys and girls?" asked Jerry, randomly.

"You can't have the girls in the same class with us, you know!" The boy behind him looked at Jerry. "Hello. I'm Roy." He grasped Jerry's hand.

"Hi Roy, I'm Jerry. Well, I don't understand that. Boys and girls are together out in the world there," he waved his arm towards the door, "and that seems to work okay."

"I don't want girls in our class. My sister is a girl and she's mean."

"But I don't understand ..."

"Stop asking questions. The nuns will beat you."

"WHAT?"

"Shhh, quiet down there!" a nun pointed at Jerry.

"Now you've done it," whispered Roy under his breath.

Jerry looked around. He felt like he did in church. Stained glass windows, a crucifix, and spaces that were much too large for little boys. He got the urge to run away again. A nun appeared out of nowhere and gripped Jerry's arms, pointing him toward another group of boys.

The nuns can read minds! Oh no! This is terrible.

The boys were shepherded into classrooms. Jerry found himself at a wooden desk about halfway back from the front of the room. There were large banks of windows along one wall, and a desk at the front. A blackboard ran the length of the front wall.

Hope I never have to go up there.

After the pledge of allegiance and prayers, the nuns began talking about the rules. They expected one hundred percent obedience from students in order to graduate them from one class to the next. Then they explained what subjects would be taught.

For the Love of an Airplane

Rather than feeling excited, Jerry felt more fear build up. He felt as if gravity had been multiplied threefold and he was stuck in it. Quicksand. It felt like a dream. He took a couple of deep breaths and tuned out. Windows ... blue sky ....

"Jerry!" He looked up to see a wooden ruler in a blur hit his knuckles as the nun loomed over him. He caught the scent of rose blossoms and antiseptic. He cried out involuntarily.

"Jerry! I asked you to tell us your father's occupation. We are getting to know each other."

"Mechanic. Mechanic. He's a mechanic at the Chrysler dealership."

"Thank you, Jerry." Sister Anne bustled off to the front of the room.

A mid-morning break came as a relief. Jerry stood up and looked for Roy. Seeing him near the back, he motioned him over, and they walked out into the hall, following the students into another room.

"See, I told you how easy it is the get in trouble."

"How do you know about all of this?" asked Jerry.

"My sister is in third grade. She told me what to expect."

"Well, I know this is only first grade, but nothing is making any sense to me. Instead of starting out with science and math, Sister Anne is talking about Mary and Jesus and the bible. I already did that in bible study at church. She is acting like these are real people."

"They are real people."

"How do you know that?"

"Because they told me that."

"That's not a good reason."

Roy shook his head. "You're confusing me, Jerry. All I can say is, if you don't believe everything and learn it, you're going to be in trouble. Big, big, trouble. Then your parents find out. My sister said so."

"It sounds like your sister is in trouble a lot."

"She is."

It was time to go back into the classroom. Jerry thought about running away again, as the fear pressed down on him. He took a deep breath and followed Roy back into class. *Don't think about running away. The nuns can read minds.*

"The reason angels can fly is because they take themselves lightly."
~G. K. Chesterton

Chapter 3

DC-3s

The 1937 green Dodge sedan lumbered down the country road towards the Rochester airport.

"We're going to have to do something about Jerry and school." Martha turned to look at Andy in the driver's seat.

"What's the problem?"

"You know what the problem is. Sister Bethany tells me that Jerry is questioning everything. He's not paying attention in class, he looks out the windows, he's self-absorbed. We held him back from first grade when he was six to get him a little more mature, but it's not working out. This is all over again, just like Holy Family. St Johns is the same story. Changing schools

For the Love of an Airplane

between first and second grade hasn't helped one bit. He's going to have to repeat the grade. Again."

It's amazing how your parents can carry on a conversation like you're not even here in the back seat, hearing every word. Maybe they forgot I'm here, thought Jerry. He shivered. The heater's warmth didn't reach into the back seat.

They entered the short tunnel under the railroad tracks. The eight-year-old gripped the window crank and armrest as they emerged on the other side, lifting up just enough to see the American Airlines DC-3 take off from runway 18. He slipped back into the seat, his eyes wide with astonishment. The aircraft thundered over the car.

"My goodness, those machines are loud," shouted Martha from the front.

"Amazing machines," said Andy. "There are dozens of passengers on that airplane. I think it can seat thirty people."

"Goodness. What is happening to the world?" Martha shook her head.

Jerry loved the trip under the railroad track and up onto the south end of the airport runway on the way to his sister's house. It was rare to see the airplanes take off over the car. This day was special. Oblivious to the conversation going on in the front seat, Jerry was thinking about airplanes. The very essence of magic, he thought. To leave the ground and go to the sky, and look down? He shut his eyes and thought about taking off from that runway. He felt his heart beat a little faster. "I'm going to fly my own airplane some day!" Jerry blurted out.

"What was that?" His mother turned around to look at Jerry.

A stab of fear struck the young boy, who, normally quite reticent, gathered up all his nerve and again shouted out, "I'm going to own and fly an airplane some day!"

Martha frowned. "Gerald Carl! That's the stupidest thing you have ever said. I don't want to ever hear that again. That is just ridiculous!" She shook her head and turned back to the front, looking at Andy. He didn't say a word.

Jerry cowered in the back. He put his hands over his eyes as tears overflowed down his cheeks. He grabbed the corner of his jacket and wiped his face.

Five minutes later, they arrived at sister Arline's house. As soon as the car stopped, Jerry opened the left side door and got out, running into the house and to the porch, where he could watch the airplanes coming and going. Jerry's heart raced as a another aircraft thundered over the house. *Two airplanes in one day!* He was excited and upset at the same time. *I will own and fly an airplane someday. I will.*

For the Love of an Airplane

Arline watched Jerry sweep through the living room and out to the porch. She didn't feel slighted; she knew the boy was in love with airplanes. *A normal child.* She smiled as Andy and Martha came through the front door with several baskets.

Jerry settled into a chair on the porch to wait for the next aircraft. A chilly wind blew through the trees, rustling the shrubs at the edge of the stone patio. He buttoned up his jacket and then pulled up the collar. He knew it would be awhile, but it was worth being patient. He heard voices inside the house. His mother was saying something to Arline.

"I think we're going to have to take Jerry out of St John's. This is only his second year of school, but he's having to repeat subjects and the nuns tell me he is disobedient."

Jerry heard a loud laugh from Arline.

"Disobedient? I can't believe that. Jerry is always kind and helpful when he's with me."

Jerry picked up the wicker chair and moved closer to the window, where he could hear better.

"He's fine at home, too," replied Martha, "but Sister Bethany tells me he keeps questioning her about his religion subjects, when he should be listening to what they are telling him. We have tried to raise all of you as participating Catholics, leading you closer to God through the holy sacraments."

Another loud guffaw came from Arline. "I feel sorry for him; I think he knows more than the nuns do."

"Arline! Stop that. You're a bad influence. You've lost your way. We did everything we could to instill Christian values and practice into your daily life, and you've rejected it. We want Jerry to be raised as a God-loving member of the Christian community."

"Then I *really* feel sorry for him. Poor Jerry," retorted Arline.

Martha put down her bundle of knitting, exasperated. "Arline, you always have been the unrepentant black sheep of the family, haven't you. Well, don't let it rub off on Jerry. He needs to complete his classes so he can navigate life."

The entire time mother and daughter were talking, Andy was reading through the newspaper, not saying a word.

"Andy!" Martha turned to him. "Put that paper down. What are we going to do about Jerry?"

Andy put the paper down with a sigh. "We should take him out of St. John's and put him into a vocational school, a technical school, someplace where he can work with his hands. He's logical. He's good with his mechanical ability and he's creative. He knows how to think things through."

"True stories are always good because they are so odd, and so unlikely."
~Steven Knight

Chapter 4

1945:
The Frigate

Somehow, turning nine years old made a difference. And so did the school. As Jerry entered public-school building #46, he felt a measure of confidence replace the fear he was so used to in catholic school. This time, after the pledge of allegiance, they got right into subjects. He knew he would need math and science, and probably some geography, if he was going to be a pilot. He didn't see where English or social studies would be of any help. Yet, if he was going to graduate, he'd need to do whatever was required. He realized that school was a series of hoops he had to jump through. He still found himself looking out the window and not paying attention. He was several years older

For the Love of an Airplane

now than the students in his class, since he'd had to repeat grades. He looked at his schedule card and saw that he needed to report to the guidance counselor's office at 9am.

He stood at the entrance to the office, waiting for the counselor to call him in. A woman at a large oak desk looked up and saw him at the door fidgeting.

"Jerry Stadtmiller?"

"Yes, yes, that's me."

"Come in and have a seat. My name is Mrs. Abercrombie. We are making up the list of students for elective subjects. So, what do you want to take this year besides the core subjects?"

"I didn't know we could choose."

"Yes, you can take art, music, creative writing, sports, or shop."

"Shop?"

"Yes, Shop. You'll learn some mechanics, woodworking, blueprint reading, metal-working, and use of tools. I teach the shop class."

"You teach Shop?" Jerry looked at Mrs. Abercrombie. He hoped she couldn't read his thoughts like the nuns did. *How does a married lady know about shop?*

"I could make something out of wood?"

"Yes, okay. I will put you in Shop. It will be the last class of the day, at 2:30pm, for ninety minutes."

"Yes, thank you, ma'am." Jerry was shy, but he was polite to a fault.

A lady who teaches Shop. This should be interesting.

The next week, Jerry sat in math class, looking out the windows and at the clock on the wall in alternating glances. When the teacher asked questions, Jerry shrank into his chair. It was very different from when he was in first grade, where he couldn't evade the overbearing nuns. But he was still frightened that the teacher would call on him. They were learning fractions. Jerry understood halves, quarters, eighths; but when the teacher started showing on the blackboard how to multiply them, Jerry stopped listening.

The bell rang. Jerry jumped out of his seat, ready for shop class.

There were nine other boys assembled in the shop room.

"Where are the girls?" Jerry asked Brett, the boy next to him.

"They take Home Economics."

"What's that?"

"Cooking, making clothes, that kind of stuff."

"Why is our shop teacher a lady when girls aren't allowed to be in this class?"

"Shh. You're asking too many questions."

Mrs. Abercrombie started class. She gave the boys a tour of the shop room, which included the tool crib, the bench tools, and the textbooks.

"If you can look information up, then you don't have to remember it. The books will explain how to measure things, and instructions for building. Today, I want you to go through the book and pick a project to work on."

For the first time, Jerry raised his hand. He couldn't believe he was doing it.

For the Love of an Airplane

"Jerry."

"Can we build anything we want?"

"Yes."

"Can I make something that is not in the project book if I want?"

"Yes."

"I would like to build a model of the frigate USS *Constitution*. I have a picture at home."

Mrs. Abercrombie stifled a laugh in front of the child, realizing that he was serious. "Yes, yes, of course you can."

The next day was Saturday. Jerry woke up thinking about his shop project. He went over to the dresser and emptied his cash jar out onto the bed.

I will have to learn how to do math, he thought. *Even fractions.*

The previous summer, Jerry had taken his wheeled wagon across the street where the old railcar factory had been. It had burned down in the middle of the night. There were still lots of bricks and blocks left in the rubble. The grout had fallen away, leaving clean and shiny bricks behind. He picked out the cleanest and nicest looking bricks to take home in his cart.

What am I going to build with these?

He got home and stacked the bricks. Then he had an idea. Why not make a fire pit? The bricks were fireproof. Then he could put sticks in the center and have his own fire. He tried it out.

The neighbor next door saw Jerry's firepit and asked him if he'd build a firepit for them. Jerry was delighted. He went back for more bricks, collecting enough to build firepits for more neighbors. He saved the money they paid him for the projects.

He looked at the contents of his jar. By his calculations, he had $2.46. He stuffed it all into his right front jeans pocket and set out, taking the bus downtown and walking into Toytown. He found several two-foot long 2x4 sections of modeler wood—balsa—string, a section of fabric for sails, three containers of enamel in different colors, and glue. It all came to $1.95. He still had to pay five cents for the bus.

Pleased that he could afford the parts, he spent the weekend gluing the wood into one piece and then carving out the detail. Then he made sails and rigging. Finally, looking at the picture he had, he painted the detail onto the ship.

On Monday, Jerry set out early with his frigate, arriving at the counselor's office before classes. Mrs. Abercrombie was sitting at her desk, just as Jerry hoped she would be. He took a deep breath.

Mrs. Abercrombie looked up from some paperwork to see Jerry's excited face and then the model ship he held in his hands.

"My word!" she exclaimed in surprise as she viewed the ship. "Come in, Jerry."

At that same moment, the school principal, Mrs. Delahanty, entered the office and saw the three-masted frigate as Jerry held it up.

The cotton cloth, glued to the string for rigging, waved slightly as the air moved in the room. The prow was carved to a point, with painted decoration accentuating the angle. Jerry reached into his back pocket for a small piece of wood shaped to form a stand for the ship. He placed it on the desk in front of Mrs. Abercrombie, carefully put the ship on the stand, and stood back.

"My goodness! Where did you get that ship?" asked Mrs. Abercrombie.

"I made it for shop class." Jerry felt fear and pride mix in front of the two women, not knowing what to say next.

"I'm amazed, Jerry. This is a beautiful ship you have crafted," said Mrs. Abercrombie. "*Old Ironsides*, launched in 1797. May I touch it?"

"Yes, of course," said Jerry, moving his weight from one foot to the other.

The two women were incredulous, mouths agape.

"Mrs. Abercrombie, I would say to you that this child deserves an A grade in his shop class for this quarter."

"And we have barely begun." said Mrs. Abercrombie.

The principal sat down in front of the ship.

Jerry was all nerves, with his hands at his side, weaving a little back and forth in anticipation, waiting for Mrs. Delahanty to speak.

"Jerry. This is stunning. Could you build another ship model for me to put in my office?"

"Ah ..." Jerry hesitated and then said, "Yes, yes, I will, I can." Jerry took a deep breath. "But, ah, I spent all my money on this one."

"I would be happy to pay for it. How much did this cost you?"

"It was expensive. It cost me two dollars if you include the bus ride."

"One moment." Mrs. Delahanty left the office and went into the room next door, and returned with two one-dollar bills.

"Here's two dollars for you. Are you sure this is enough?"

"Yes, it is," Jerry said, a mixture of nerves and excitement in his voice.

Mrs. Abercrombie was still examining the detail on the ship.

"Very well done, Jerry. Very well done."

Jerry stood in front of the two women, took another deep breath, and broke into a broad smile of relief.

That semester Jerry got Math—D, Science—C, Reading—D, Writing—D, and Shop—A.

It was a beginning.

"The greatest mistake you can make in life is to be continually fearing you will make one."
~Elbert Hubbard

Chapter 5

1952: Baseball

One day in English class, the teacher told the students to read one of the ten books she listed on the blackboard. Then she pointed to a stack of books on the table. "Pick one out. Then in two weeks, you'll do a book report to the rest of the class."

A lightning bolt of fear caught Jerry by surprise. *In front of the class?* He shut his eyes. *Oh no. In front of the class?* He caught his breath and looked at the list. *Nothing here about airplanes. Nothing. What am I going to do? I won't think about it.*

Days went by. The wall of fear grew higher and higher as Jerry put off picking out a book. *I'll fail. But I need to graduate.* He couldn't repeat another grade or he would be too far behind. *What will I do?* He felt ill.

Three days before the book report was due, he snuck up to the table after class and grabbed the first book he saw. When he got back out into the hall, he held it up to look. *Baseball? I don't know anything about baseball.*

He was a slow reader and spent several nights with the book. He finished the book the day before class. The next morning, he entered the classroom at the last minute. *I'll sit in the back; she won't see me.* He tried to make himself as small and inconspicuous as he could as the class settled down. Suddenly, it was silent. Mrs. Jennette entered the classroom and looked around. Most of the students were squirming, looking down, hoping they wouldn't be called on. *They feel the same way I do.*

"Jerry Stadtmiller. You are first," said Mrs. Jennette.

Oh, no! How could it be? What did I do to deserve this?

Jerry's stomach turned over, and dread filled every crevice in his body. Did he really hear his name? She must have made a mistake.

"Jerry!" Mrs. Jennette raised her voice and looked at him. "Now, please."

Jerry stood up, hearing his chair scrape loudly against the old wood floor. All eyes were on him as he made his way slowly to the front of the classroom. He stood in front of the blackboard, clutching the baseball book. He took a deep breath.

"Ah, this book is about a bunch of kids who were poor. They were poor, and they wanted, uh, they liked to play baseball together in the neighborhood." He stopped for a moment. *It's like my mind just went blank. What am I supposed to say?* Every other student was looking at him, some were making faces. *They are taunting me.*

"Yes? Go on," said Mrs. Jennette.

Jerry took a deep breath. "Okay, so they wanted to play baseball, but they had to make the baseballs because they didn't have any. They didn't have the money to buy them in the store new. So the team leader, his name was Shago, made the baseballs for the team. He made them out of tightly wadded paper covered with leather and sewn with string."

Jerry paused. His heart was shaking in his chest. The students were looking at him, and Tom, in the back, was making silly faces. *Don't look at him.*

"So, they were getting ready to play a baseball game at school and they were practicing. One teacher gave the team a real baseball, and it was a brand new one, from a store. But the pitcher for the team didn't like the new ball, so he went back to playing with Shago's balls."

The entire classroom burst instantly into raucous laughter. Jerry's face turned bright red; he gasped uncontrollably. There was nothing the teacher could do as the boys continued out of control, with laugher and desk banging, foot stomping, and twittering noises.

Jerry placed the book on the table, and with his head lowered, found his way back to the desk at the back. He put his arms on the desk and put his head down on his arms. He was shaking. The embarrassment continued to send blood boiling through his face and neck. He felt nauseous.

For the Love of an Airplane

"STOP!" Finally, Mrs. Jennette's voice overcame the roar. "Stop! Quiet!" she said again. The laughter dropped off. The students were wiping tears from their eyes, some still turned around to look at Jerry.

"Jerry."

Oh no, what now?

"Jerry, thank you for that book report. Stanley Evans, you are next."

The class quieted as the next student got up. Jerry left his head resting on his arms on the desk, waiting for the blood to drain. *I will never, ever, do that again in my life, so help me God.*

Jerry's parents recognized his fears, but could do little about it except hope that it would fade with time and accomplishment. They enrolled him in Boy Scouts.

"Jerry, you'll enjoy meeting other boys your age and being part of a social group," his dad said. "Mr. Adams runs the troop, and they hold the meetings at the Parker building down the street, just a few blocks away."

"Okay."

The first meeting night, Jerry forced himself to go to the meeting, terrified. He was quiet and observant, noting the meeting schedule. The following week, he left the house on time.

"This is a good sign," Andy said to Martha.

"It is. I hope it helps him," said Martha.

Later that night, Jerry returned.

"How was the meeting?" asked his dad.

"Okay."

"That's it?"

"Yep."

Andy shook his head and looked at Martha. When Jerry left the room, he said, "We've done all we can."

The next week, when Andy saw the scoutmaster, Mr. Adams, he asked how Jerry was doing.

"We haven't seen him since the first meeting."

"Life is really simple, but we insist on making it complicated."
~ Confucius

Chapter 6

Engines

Ninth grade started like the others, but with a different guidance counselor. Mr. Peabody invited Jerry in to the office. He pointed to the worn oak chair on rollers in front of his desk. Jerry sat down, the old tilt springs complaining for grease.

"Jerry. Welcome. I'm Mr. Peabody, the guidance counselor for the high school. You've had a tough time in school, I see, but you're persevering. There's value in that. I'm going to tell you to keep at it. We want to do two things. The first is to give you a well-rounded education so that you can go get a good job for yourself. The second is to open up a line of possibility for you to discover what you're good at and what you enjoy. If you can find these two things—good at something you enjoy—and have the discipline to learn, you will be successful."

For the Love of an Airplane

Jerry would normally tune out the adults in his life out of fear. But something resonated with Mr. Peabody. Mr. Peabody cared. He sat up straighter in the squeaking chair and rolled a little closer to the desk.

"There are subjects you need to master in high school, and you will have these as core curriculum. They include math and science, English and writing, and history and social studies, and geography. You can pick a major—the subject you like the most—and the others will be built around it. We have math, science, English, history, and aviation. Which one would you like to major in?"

"Aviation?"

"Yes, aviation. We added it this year. It's a growing field with great potential. We're so close to the airport, and the airport is growing fast. With an aviation major, you can pilot for the airlines, work as a mechanic on airplanes, work at the airport in administration, or teach aviation."

Jerry felt that same thrill in his chest as he did when he spotted the airplane take off and fly over the car. He was transported to the future. *A pilot? A mechanic? He could be paid to do these things?*

"Jerry." Mr. Peabody was looking at him. "You're daydreaming."

"Oh, sorry! I was thinking about that. About aviation."

"Do you want to major in aviation, then?"

"Yes! Yes, I do, please sir."

A week later, Jerry was renewing his efforts in class, knowing that he now had a goal. Instead of looking out the windows at blue sky and thinking about being out there, he opened his books and listened to the teacher. He had a notepad and pencil. But he couldn't wait for his first aviation class. He kept flipping his attention from the science text to the clock on the wall. *This is hard.*

The bell rang, and he got to the aviation classroom early. He picked a seat in the front. *I can't believe it. I'm sitting in the front row.* The room smelled like shop, only better. He could smell oil and diesel fuel. The room was connected to a large garage-type space that eventually would have airplanes and airplane parts. He saw engines on stands in the back of the room.

Edison Tech Aviation Class

Jerry is second from the left

For the Love of an Airplane

A middle-aged man walked in with a briefcase. *That must be the instructor.* He put his case on the desk in front and then wrote his name on the blackboard. *Ernest Wood.* Eleven other students filed in. Mr. Wood looked around and waited for the class to settle down. Like shop class, it was the last session of the day, leaving time for extra activities after class.

Mr. Wood began talking about the history of aviation. Jerry was enthralled.

"This class is about aviation; it won't teach you how to fly, but it will teach you about the history and the manufacturing of airplanes and how they work. You'll learn how to work on airplanes and engines. You'll learn the science of flight, and you'll learn about all the jobs you can apply for when you graduate. Whether you want to give directions to pilots from a tower, fix engines, go into pilot or mechanic training, or jockey paperwork, you're in the right place. Airplanes are the future."

Jerry made notes on his pad of paper. *I'm going to have to learn how to write faster,* he thought.

"Let's switch gears," said Mr. Wood. "Look at the engines lined up against the wall in back of the classroom." He pointed to the back of the room, near the double doors to the garage.

"Here's your assignment. Write the name of every engine you see here—there are eight of them, along with the horsepower. The placards are below each one with specifications on it. Tomorrow, if you can point to each one and tell me the full name without looking at the placards, I'll give you an A in week one of the class."

He listened intently as Mr. Wood went to the back and named them all, along with the model and the horsepower. Jerry didn't need to write the engines down. They lodged in his memory.

The next day, Jerry was ready.

Mr. Wood asked, "Who can get up in front of the class and recite the engines?"

Get up in front of the class? No way, thought Jerry. He felt crushed. Elation and dread washed over him. In his mind's eye, he reeled off the engines to himself, mouthing the names under his breath. *Pratt & Whitney R1830, Rolls-Royce/Packard Merlin/V-1650, Allison V-1710, Curtis Conqueror...* he knew he had them all.

"No one can recite the engines?" Mr. Wood looked around. Jerry shrank back, hoping Mr. Wood would not call on him. The other boys did the same, looking down at the floor and shuffling their feet. Jerry shut his eyes. *Not again.*

"Well, okay, no one gets an A. Let's move on."

Mr. Wood picked back up where he'd left off the day before, talking about the history of aviation. He wrote the dates and events on the blackboard, and Jerry wrote everything down.

When the class let out, Mr. Wood stopped Jerry as he was walking out.

"Jerry, I know you are shy. I can see it. But I could also see you mouthing the engine models. You know every one of them, don't you?"

"Yes, sir."

For the Love of an Airplane

"Can you tell me what they are right now?"

"Yes, sir." Jerry walked over to the wall. Pointing to each engine without looking at the placard, he recited each engine's name, model, and horsepower perfectly. Then he sighed in relief, as if he were catching his breath.

Mr. Wood smiled. "You get an A. You're going to do well. You will teach others one day. I'm going to help you. Confidence comes when you know something inside out."

In that moment, life changed for Jerry.

"You are exactly where you need to be."
~Unknown

Chapter 7

Line Boy

"I have an announcement. Listen up." Mr. Wood waited for the class to settle down. "There's an opening at the airport for a line boy. If you're interested, get over there after class lickety-split and apply."

Jerry turned to his friend Jay at the next desk. "What's a line boy?"

Mr. Wood heard Jerry's question.

"A line boy does the important odd jobs around the airport. They fuel aircraft, tie down aircraft, clean aircraft, and do minor repairs with oversight from a licensed mechanic. The pay is minimal, but it includes an hour of flight instruction every week."

Jerry's eyes widened in surprise. "You mean flying-an-airplane-kind of instruction? You get to touch a real airplane?" The class laughed, but it was all in fun.

For the Love of an Airplane

Mr. Wood went on. "Yes. It's after classes during the week, with Friday off, and all-day Saturday and Sunday. You'll need to be disciplined about your schoolwork." He looked at Jerry.

Jerry smiled. He couldn't wait to get to the airport. Mr. Wood began talking about horsepower and fuel burn, but Jerry was thinking about flying. It took forever for the bell to ring.

After class let out, he took the bus to the city line and walked the two miles to the airport. He walked into the office and up to the desk, where there was a stern-looking woman with jet black hair tied back in a bun.

"I'm here to apply for the line boy job."

"Hello. I'm Anna, Mr. Stopplebeiner's assistant. Did Mr. Wood direct you here?"

"Yes."

"Can you show up reliably every day except Fridays?"

"Why can't I come on Friday?"

Anna laughed, which surprised Jerry. "Well, okay. We'll show you what you need to know. The pay is $4.89 a week. You'll get an hour and a half of flight instruction in a PA-11 thrown in."

"Flight instruction? Great, that's great!" Jerry felt like he'd arrived in heaven. *Flight instruction? Am I dreaming?*

Anna turned to the room behind her. "Jim, we filled the position. Please get Mr. Stadtmiller a logbook."

Jim Weir, the flight instructor, came out of the back room with a pilot's logbook in a hard black cover. "Be sure to put your name in the front." He shook Jerry's hand and gave him the logbook.

Jerry felt like he'd been given a twenty-dollar bill. He took the logbook and caressed the leather cover. "Thank you, thank you," he stammered in excitement.

Jerry walked out of the office floating on air. He couldn't wait to get home and tell his parents, especially his dad, about his first job.

The next day, he was walking down the corridor when Mr. Peabody, the guidance counselor, waved him into the office.

He pointed to the chair. Jerry sat down, suddenly worried.

"I see your grades are coming up. I talked to Mr. Wood, and he told me you are a natural in aviation. When Mr. Wood says something like that about a student, it means a lot. Mr. Wood also told me you'll be taking a job as a line boy at the airport. I know you will enjoy that, given your interest in aviation.

Since you're enjoying your aviation class, I'd like to point out that a renewed effort in your other classes will drive your success in aviation. To be a pilot, mechanic, or engineer you'll need math and science, and of course you can't navigate life without good reading and writing skills. I just wanted to point that out in case it had escaped you.

"Right now, you're getting A's in aviation, but C's in your other subjects. I hope that your time at the airport does not jeopardize your progress in your other subjects."

Jerry sat up straight in the old chair as it creaked. He realized that Mr. Peabody was right. "Yes sir, I will renew my effort."

"Good. It's a lot to think about. Thanks for coming in."

For the Love of an Airplane

Jerry felt the weight of expectations on him, but he also felt that he could do the work and study too, as long as he remembered the end goal: to fly an airplane. *To own and fly an airplane.*

He couldn't sleep that night. The next day, his classes seemed to drag on and on. All he could think about was getting out to the airport. When the bell finally rang, he hustled out in relief, taking the bus to the city line and walking the rest of the way to the airport.

He walked into the flight office. His boss, Carl Stopplebeiner, and the flight instructor, Jim, were sitting behind the counter, talking. Stopplebeiner looked up.

"Hey kid, Jim got you your logbook, I see. We can do some flying later. Here, come out now and help me get the Tri-pacer going. Jim, I'm flying over to Spencerport for that FAA paperwork we need. I'll be back in an hour."

Jerry followed Mr. Stopplebeiner outside. He seemed to be a gruff, unhappy old man without smile muscles. He got into the airplane with Jerry standing there, not knowing what to do.

"Hey kid, okay, pull the prop through."

"Do what?"

"Pull the propeller through."

Why is he asking me to pull the prop?

"Is there a switch?" Jerry shouted.

"Yeah, yeah, pull it through," Stopplebeiner shouted from the cockpit.

I don't think he hears me.

Jerry remembered seeing how this was done in a movie. You grab the propeller blade and push it down and around. That starts the airplane. It should be easy. This would be fun. He walked up to the front of the plane and grabbed the tip of the top blade.

"Which way?"

Stopplebeiner pointed to Jerry's left. Jerry grasped the blade at the top and pulled it down. It wasn't easy, like he thought it would be. Stopplebeiner looked at him expectantly. At five foot seven inches tall and 140 pounds, Jerry was light and lean for his age. He decided to throw himself into the effort.

Jim Weir looked up from his desk and out the office window and gasped. Old Stopplebeiner was going to kill this new line boy. He jumped up to run outside. In that moment, he saw Jerry give a heave to the prop with his shoulder. The engine started, the propeller missing the boy by an inch, if that. Jerry fell backwards onto the pavement in the excitement. He heard Stopplebeiner swearing. Jerry crawled to his left, clear of the spinning prop, and stood up, slapping his trousers to get the dirt off.

"Get in, kid! Get in!" cried the old man over the engine noise. Jerry's eyes went wide, and he stumbled over to the right side of the airplane and got into the front right seat.

"Buckle in, kid, buckle in."

Jim watched them taxi off, shaking his head.

What in the world was Stopplebeiner thinking? He must feel bad about nearly killing this new kid.

For the Love of an Airplane

Rochester Airport, 1950
New York

"Happiness is a butterfly, which when pursued, is always just beyond your grasp, but which, if you will sit down quietly, may alight upon you."
~Nathaniel Hawthorne

Chapter 8

First Flight

He was in an airplane.
I am inside a real flying machine.

Jerry forgot all about the prop incident as they taxied away from the flight office. Stopplebeiner stopped short of the runway and ran the engine RPM up. Jerry watched him flip switches and move the controls. Stopplebeiner picked up a microphone to his left and talked into it. Jerry knew it was to the airport tower, but he couldn't understand what they were saying.

I will have to learn how to talk on the radio. How do you hear anything over the engine?

They taxied on to the runway. Jerry felt the power of the Lycoming 0-290 build as it propelled the small airplane faster and faster. The pavement and landscape began to blur. The exhilaration was breathtaking. This was better than Jerry's wildest flying dreams. He soaked in the sounds of the engine and air noise. It was so loud and so wonderful. All the while, Stopplebeiner didn't say a word. Jerry felt like he was the only one in the airplane.

They lifted off the runway. It felt like being in an anti-gravity ship, as if the earth was pushing them up. Jerry was spellbound as he gazed out the side window. Cool air rushed through the cockpit. The landscape unfolded, with roadways and fields stretched out everywhere before them. Small ponds and lakes appeared to the side, the surface glistening under the bright sun like metallic silver discs. As they climbed, the landscape became a patchwork of neat rectangular fields and intersecting roads full of color and texture.

Wow. I need to pinch myself. Is this a dream? Gotta be a dream.

"Hey kid … what's your name? Gerald?" Stopplebeiner shouted over the din.

"Jerry, I'm Jerry."

"Okay, Jerry, this is your first airplane ride?"

"Yes, Sir."

"Here, take the controls."

Jerry's heart leaped as he placed his hands tentatively on the control yoke in front of him. Over the next fifteen minutes, Stopplebeiner showed Jerry what the controls did and what the instruments were. Jerry soaked it up. Stopplebeiner pointed out the rudder pedals at his feet.

"Rudder is really important," said Stopplebeiner. "It's as important as the ailerons. Push and see what it does."

Jerry wasn't sure what Stopplebeiner meant with the words, but he got the message. He pushed in on the left pedal and felt the craft yaw to the left. He pulled back on the control yoke, feeling the airplane slow and climb.

"Okay, I have the airplane," said Stopplebeiner. They were approaching Spencerport.

They landed at Spencerport on a grass strip and taxied up to a small building. A young man came running out, and avoiding the whirring prop, passed an envelope in to Stopplebeiner.

"Thanks Arnie, see you," shouted Mr. Stopplebeiner.

They taxied back out and lined up on the grass strip. They took off to the east. Once again, anti-gravity in action, the sky was pulling the little airplane into her element, thought Jerry. The quilting patterns of the earth, the glistening of the sun off water, and the cloud layers appeared in enhanced 3D contrast. He hoped they would never land.

So much more than I thought it would be.

They approached the Rochester airport and lined up with the runway. There were many runways. It looked like a geometry puzzle. It was a stunning view out the front of the airplane, as if the engine were eating up the ground as they dropped lower. Jerry felt they were going too fast, but as they floated over the pavement, Mr. Stopplebeiner pulled gently on the control yoke and the tires squeaked as they met the runway.

Mr. Stopplebeiner pulled off at an intersection and stopped the airplane, turning to Jerry. "Kid, remember this about landing. Don't stop flying the airplane when you're on the ground. Keep control until you are all the way back to the hangar. Here,

For the Love of an Airplane

I'll show you how to taxi and where the controls should be, depending on the wind. Never forget this one thing, or you'll have an accident."

Jerry was euphoric, at a loss for words.

Back inside the office, Stopplebeiner asked Jerry for his logbook. Jerry pulled it out of his book bag and handed it over. "Okay, your first flight. We will put it in here." Stopplebeiner filled out the details standing at the counter and handed it back to Jerry, all the while still not smiling once.

"You might be pilot material," he said matter-of-factly, with the same grim look on his face.

But Jerry looked like he had been introduced to an angel. His eyes were full of excitement. Jim Weir looked over at Jerry and smiled, knowing he'd been bitten by the aircraft bug. Forever.

"Expect problems and eat them for breakfast."
~Alfred A. Montapert

Chapter 9

1953: The Accident

The first year working at the airport did wonders for Jerry's shy streak and for his grades in school. Once he realized he was good at something, confidence flowed in. He learned to fly, got his private pilot license, and was working on flight ratings. He also took a liking to history, since much of it included airplanes.

As much as he loved piloting, he enjoyed repairs and maintenance even more. He could hear an engine and tell you what it was. He was always thinking about what he could do with airplane parts. He thought of his dad, who he knew could listen to a car engine when it came in for service and tell you what was wrong with it.

One day at the airport, he looked out in the field at several Fairchild PT-26 airplanes that had been junked. Teak and spruce had rotted through and the fabric was in tatters.

For the Love of an Airplane

I wonder if they might sell me one of those, Jerry thought. He decided to talk to Jim Weir.

"Well, I don't see why not," said Jim. "They're just rotted junk. They've been sitting there for months. I'll ask."

The next day, Jim had good news for Jerry. "Yes, you can have a PT-26."

"How much?"

"Nothing. They'll be happy you're hauling it away. Eddie wants to know where to drag it to."

"How about to my backyard?"

"What are you going to do with it?"

"Ah, I'm not sure. Rebuild it?"

Jim laughed. "Yeah, right."

You'd surmise that Jerry's parents would think there was something odd about a guy with a truck and trailer dropping off a derelict PT-26 airplane in the backyard of their home. Yet they didn't seem to think that was anything out of the ordinary for Jerry. Jerry was industrious and always had a project underway. Since his grades had come up, and he had a job, they didn't bother him or interfere with his activities.

One day, Jerry's dad asked him if he wanted to get his driver's license.

"You could drive the Dodge if you need to."

"What for?" replied Jerry. "Cars are expensive. This way I can save for an airplane."

His dad smiled. "Fine with me."

"Don't tell that to Mom."

"I won't."

A week after the PT-26 had been delivered, Jerry decided to take it apart. His friend Larry offered to help him.

"I guess you know what you're doing," said Larry.

"Not really. I'll just take it apart and see what everything is. Then maybe I can put it back together. At least we'll learn something."

"Where are your tools?"

"I don't have any tools. Well, a hammer and a screwdriver. Pliers. And one adjustable wrench. These boards here will be leverage; and we can use the blocks." He pointed to the lumber he'd stacked up in the corner.

Jerry still had a good supply of cement blocks from his fire-pit building days. He stacked some up and put a few of the boards on them. "We'll take the landing gear off first. So I'll pick up the front of the fuselage until the gear slides out, then you grab the gear and move it out of the way. Then I'll set the airplane down on these blocks."

"But the engine is still on it. Won't that be a little heavy?"

"I know. But it's not that far. Like a couple of inches? We can still leverage it up."

For the Love of an Airplane

"Like I said, I figure you know what you're doing," said Larry.

Jerry got under the airplane and tried to lift it with the back of his shoulders. It wouldn't budge.

"Gosh. I only need an inch or two." Jerry shook his head while Larry looked on expectantly.

Jerry tried again. The front of the airplane lifted about a quarter of an inch.

"Well, gee, it doesn't need to go far! Let me try that again."

Jerry gathered all his strength, took a deep breath and then exhaled, and then put his back under the airplane again and heaved. The fuselage lifted another quarter of an inch, the gear slid out, and the airplane came down with Jerry under it, smashing the support blocks to bits as it hit the ground.

Jerry was stunned as the front of the airplane came down, trapping him under it. It happened so fast he felt no fear. As his body hit the loose dirt, he wondered how far down the fuselage would push him. *That was a mistake*, he thought, and in that instant waited for the airplane to squeeze the life out of him. He felt a crushing pressure on his lower back, then something sprang back. The stubs from the gear hit the ground, dug into the sand, and stopped, leaving three inches of clearance between Jerry and the engine.

Jerry gasped for a breath. *That was so fast. Is it going to come down farther? I'm still breathing.*

Larry was jumping up and down in front of him. "Oh, no! oh no! Oh no! Jerry, can you crawl out of there? Jerry? Jerry? Are you alive? Jerry?"

"Wait, Larry, wait. Let me catch my breath." *I need to crawl out from under,* he thought. *But I'm fine. Thank God. I better get out, it might fall some more.*

"Oh my God, you're alive!" Larry was still jumping up and down in front of him and hopping from one foot to the other.

"Settle down, Larry, settle down. Wait a minute. Wait."

Jerry moved his arms and then tried moving his legs to get some traction in the dirt. As his arms flailed, he was motionless from the waist down. There was no sensation at all. No pain, nothing.

I can't move!

"I can't move, Larry, I can't move my legs. I can't feel anything in my legs. Not a tingle, no pain, nothing. Are they still there?"

"Mother of Jesus, you're paralyzed! You're paralyzed! Let me go get your mother!"

"No! No! Don't! She'll holler at me. I'll be in big trouble. Pull me out of here, quick."

Larry grabbed Jerry's arms and dragged him from under the airplane. A few inches of clearance had saved him from being crushed. Larry sat down on the ground, panting. "This isn't good, this isn't good. Oh my God, let me get an ambulance for you."

"No, not yet, not yet. Larry, settle down!"

Larry was apoplectic. "We have to do something. You're hurt."

"Just wait, will you?" *I need to settle down myself.*

Jerry closed his eyes and tried to feel his lower body. Nothing. He took a deep breath. *At least I can breathe,* he thought.

"I'm waiting," said Larry, matter-of-factly.

A minute went by. "I'm waiting," said Larry again.

For the Love of an Airplane

"That's fine. Just wait, will you."

About five more minutes passed. It felt like forever. Jerry kept breathing deeply as fear coursed through him and he thought of his future in a wheelchair. *Not in an airplane*, he thought. *One more deep breath. Try to move your legs.*

"Okay, that's it. I'm going for help," said Larry.

"Wait, Larry, wait, I feel a tingling." Did he? Yes, he did. A slight prickly feeling.

Another few minutes brought returning sensation to Jerry's legs. He tried to move them.

"I'm trying to move them."

"Wiggle your left foot."

Jerry wiggled his left foot.

"I see it! I see it!" Larry was as relieved as Jerry was.

As Jerry began moving, there was an intense, stabbing pain across his lower back. He gasped as he moved to turn over. He waited.

After another few minutes, Jerry rolled over and sat up.

"Oh My God, Mother of Jesus," said Larry.

"Stop swearing like that, Larry."

"I can't help it. You almost got killed. With me helping."

"If opportunity doesn't knock, build a door."
~Milton Berle

Chapter 10

1954: The Cub

With Jerry's passion around all things aviation, his performance in high school steadily improved. He connected mathematics and science with the dynamics of flight. He connected writing with his documenting of flight maintenance and activities, and history with the development of airplanes and their success in the world wars. He moved into 11th grade.

He soloed when he was 16 years old, received his Private Pilot's license at 17 years old, completed his Commercial Pilot's license at 18, and was now working on his multi-engine and instrument qualifications.

"I need an airplane," Jerry said to his friend Alan one day as they were walking between classes.

Alan laughed and shook his head. "Right, of course you do. You don't need an airplane; you need a car. What are you going to do with an airplane? It's pretty hard to take your girlfriend to the drive-in movies in an airplane."

"I don't care about taking girls to the drive-in. It's expensive."

"And flying isn't?"

"Not if I can get my own plane instead of renting one."

"You have your auto license, right?"

"No, not yet. Airplanes first."

Jerry was in the airport office working through a maintenance procedures manual when a young man in his mid-30's walked in.

"You know anyone who could go in on a Piper J-3 Cub?" the man said to Jim Weir behind the counter.

"Nope. I'll keep it in mind though," replied Jim.

"Wait, wait," said Jerry, looking up from his books. "A Cub? You're looking for a Cub?"

"Yes. My name is William. I've found a good 1946 Piper J-3 for sale. I need a partner. But I need someone who can work on it. I'd like to fly, but I don't know a thing about the mechanicals. It'll be too expensive to pay for a shop to keep it up."

Jerry's heart rate quickened. "How much are we talking about? A good-condition Cub is probably $550 or $600."

"Five hundred and fifty."

"So, you need a partner? If I went in on this with you, how often could I fly it?"

William paused and then said, "Every day if you want. I want to fly once a week—get lessons in it, you know. But if you did, you would pay your fuel and you would keep it flying?"

"Yes sir, yes, sir. When do you need the money?"

"Sometime this coming week?"

"You have a deal!"

The two men shook hands. After William walked out of the office, Jerry sat down. He was trembling. He'd been saving every paycheck from the airport. Now he knew why. He took a deep breath. *I'm going to own an airplane.*

For the Love of an Airplane

Jerry flew the Cub every chance he got. It was in good condition, and he lavished attention on it. William was delighted with the arrangement.

At school, Alan kept ribbing him about not having a car.

"I can't believe it. You own an airplane and not a car! You will not find a girl to get in that airplane with you."

"Who says?"

"Says me," Alan replied.

Jerry sighed. "Girls are expensive, and cars are expensive. The Cub costs me a little more than a dollar an hour. I can't have everything. And as for girls not wanting to fly, I bet you our English teacher, Mrs. Barkley, would get in the Cub. She's said as much."

"No way!"

The next day, Jerry approached Mrs. Barkley.

"Were you serious when you said you wanted a flight in the Cub?" asked Jerry.

"I was indeed serious. But I'd better check with my husband and with your aviation teacher if you invite me. I think it would be absolutely thrilling. I've never been in an airplane."

The following week, Mrs. Barkley showed up at the airport with her husband and three small children.

"I checked with your aviation teacher, Mr. Wood, and he said that you are a very conscientious and safe pilot. That was reassuring," said Mrs. Barkley.

"Would your kids like to go after you? Or your husband?"

"No, no, thank you. They aren't too excited about it."

Jerry explained the procedures for starting and got Mrs. Barkley into the rear seat and comfortable. Mrs. Barkley's husband,

Jim, took some photographs. The children wanted to get into the airplane too. They all laughed as the kids pouted on the ground, watching the airplane taxi away.

Jerry took Mrs. Barkley on a thirty-minute tour of the Rochester countryside. She kept talking the whole time, excited. Jerry couldn't hear a word she was saying.

When they returned, Mrs. Barkley exited the airplane, giddy. "That was wonderful!" she said to Jerry, with her family looking on. "That was the most wonderful thing I've ever done! Thank you Jerry, thank you so much." Mrs. Barkley even hugged him.

He still got a C in English.

For the Love of an Airplane

"That's what children are for - that their parents may not be bored."
~Ivan Turgenev

Chapter 11

Dad

Jerry got home from the airport one night as the school year was wrapping up. His dad came over to him. He placed his hand on Jerry's shoulder and squeezed it.

"Jerry, I'm so proud of what you've done with school and the job at the airport. You know, as you were growing up, we were concerned because you were born so early, but you've really applied yourself in the face of challenges. You know your mother cares and loves you, but you wouldn't know it. She won't show it. I wanted to let you know we have been watching and hoping, and it looks like you're doing just fine.

We're pleased that you joined the National Guard, too. That's excellent experience for you, and you may be fortunate enough to not fight in any wars. Your brother Glenn can tell you all about that. It sure mans you up fast, I'll say that, but war is dreadful. You were smart to choose the aircraft and avionics side of the Guard. You'll enjoy that."

Andy looked at Jerry and laughed. "We did everything we could to get you into Boy Scouts, but you kept doubling back here to the house. I suspected as much. Well, that's all in the past. I want you to know how proud and pleased I am with your accomplishments."

"Thanks, Dad." Jerry was embarrassed. He could feel his face flush. His parents rarely showed any emotion toward him. He knew they cared. His dad, especially, was interested in his activities and the airplanes he dragged home since they were both mechanics. In another universe, Jerry was convinced his dad would be an aircraft mechanic.

"I heard your English teacher even came out for a ride last week."

"She did. But it didn't help my grade!"

They laughed together.

"Jerry, your mother and I are making our summer trip up to Bill and Jack's next week. I know you're busy, but you know you're welcome if you can come up for a day or two. That will be an easy trip for you in the Cub."

"I will, Dad, I will."

"Dad?"

"Yes?"

"Mom knows I got the airplane. And she knows I'm a pilot. Has she said anything about that?"

"Son, don't take this the wrong way. Your mother loves you. But she thinks you're in danger when you get in the airplane, so she doesn't say anything. There's nothing to be done about that; I know you are an excellent pilot and you have a good airplane. I'm proud of you. I know your mother is also proud of you. She just won't tell you."

"Okay. I figured. Thanks, Dad, thanks."

The talk pleased Jerry. It was hard to know sometimes what your parents think about what you're doing. Jerry looked up to his dad and the short but revealing talk meant everything to him.

For the Love of an Airplane

The next week, Jerry flew up to the islands. The trip from the airport was less than an hour. It was a beautiful spring day, and Jerry felt the same magic on this trip as he did every time he got in his Cub. He and the machine were one unit, flying through a bright blue sky with fluffy white clouds above, and a gentle caressing breeze holding the airplane. He landed on a grass strip near Bill's place. He smelled freshly mown grass and hay. Brother Bill was 20 years older than Jerry. He owned a fishing resort in the Thousand Islands with a partner. He taught Jerry everything he knew about boats and fishing.

Bill was waiting there on the field with his old Ford pickup, with Sandy, the English Spaniel. Sandy jumped out of the truck and ran over to the airplane, excited to see Jerry. The small dog jumped into the rear seat of the Cub. Jerry laughed at the little dog. "Wait, San, not now, later, okay?"

Jerry and Sandy walked over to the truck and got in. Bill had a somber expression on his face. Jerry immediately knew something was wrong.

"I have some bad news for you, Jer. Dad had a heart attack. He's at the hospital. We'll go there now."

Jerry gasped. "No!"

"He's recovering. But the doctor said it's only a matter of time before he has another one. It's a blockage in an artery."

The hospital was minutes away. River hospital was just that—a hospital in the Thousand Islands on a river. Andy was in a double room on the river side with large plate-glass windows. The other bed was empty. As the two sons walked in, Sandy was quick to jump up on the bed to comfort Andy.

"Hey, Sandy!" said Andy. "Glad you brought him. A little bundle of fun, she is."

As they sat in the room talking, Jerry noticed the window faced the widest portion of the river. He got an idea.

"Dad, before I leave tomorrow to go home, I'll fly my Cub past your window. Watch for me."

"That would be great son, that would be wonderful to see," said Andy.

Nurses came in to the room and tried to shoo the dog away, but then fell for her. "Too much excitement!" said one of the nurses. "But okay, I guess he's good therapy."

After a short visit, Bill and Jerry left to go back to the rooms at the resort. There wasn't much to be done except make Andy comfortable. They got back in the truck. Sandy snuggled up to Jerry on the front bench seat.

"That was such a surprise. Dad's been so healthy over the years, it's hard to think he would have heart problems. But, he's kind of getting up there in years at 55."

"I know. Before I leave to go back, I'll fly past his window," said Jerry. "He should enjoy that."

"I know he will."

For the Love of an Airplane

The next day, Jerry did exactly that. He flew the Cub past the hospital window twice, rocking his wings. The second time, his dad was at the window, waving back.

That was the last time Jerry saw him.

"Being courageous does not mean never being scared; it means acting as you know you must even though you are undeniably afraid."
~Archbishop Desmond Tutu

Chapter 12

1955: The Fire

It was a bright and cold fall day in Western New York. The air moved crisply through dying leaves. Eddies of crinkled color moved by an invisible hand at the bases of trees paused as if to consider a different path, then started a swirling dance again. At the airport, pilots were pulling out the small airplanes in anticipation of flying again one last time before the winter cold.

Russell arrived on his bicycle, parking it against the hanger.

"Thanks for doing this, Jerry. It's so much fun to get in a flight, and even better that we have this beautiful brilliant landscape today. I brought my brand-new Leica M3, with Kodak color 35mm film. Can you believe it? With all the light today, I should get some good pictures of the countryside, even though we'll be bumping along."

For the Love of an Airplane

Jerry looked at the camera intently. "I've never seen anything like that," he said. "And color film?"

"It cost as much as your airplane, I bet." Russell pointed to the Cub. "Three hundred and forty-five dollars."

"My word! I'd rather own the airplane than the camera. Let's go."

They took off to the south. Jerry flew low over the rolling hills with a colorful panorama of fields and farms on display. As they approached Wellsville, they noticed a barn with white smoke billowing out of the open hay door. A farmhouse was about 300 feet down the hill from it.

"A fire! The barn's on fire! Hold on, Russ, I'm going to buzz the house to let them know."

Jerry flew the Cub low over the house, hoping someone would hear the airplane and come out. Nothing. He could see flames begin to travel up one side of the barn as he did a 360-degree turn to come back over the farmhouse. He lowered the nose of the Cub and flew over the house again, getting as low as he could get without endangering anyone.

Finally, they saw a woman come out the front door of the farmhouse. She looked up at the little airplane and then over at the barn and saw the smoke billowing out of the upper hay door. She waved at the Cub and ran to the barn. She opened the main doors. Two horses ran out, and she disappeared inside.

"Uh oh!" cried Russell.

Then they saw two cars roll out the door and coast slowly down a short hill and stop at a berm. The woman emerged from the door, coughing, and ran back to the house.

"I hope she called the fire department."

With nothing left to do, Jerry started flying south. They could have landed the Cub on the road to the house, but there was little they could have done about the fire.

"Getting good pictures?" asked Jerry.

"Yes, but I used all the film up on the barn fire," shouted Russell.

As they flew back over the farmhouse, they saw an antique firetruck coming up the valley. They looked at where the barn had been. There was nothing left of it. The two horses were down the hill with the antique cars, eating grass as if nothing had happened.

The woman was standing outside, her long brown hair waving in the breeze, waiting for the firetruck. She waved to the two boys in appreciation.

"If that firetruck ever arrives, it won't have anything to do," said Russell.

Five years later, Jerry was working in an aviation maintenance shop in south Florida. A customer was hanging around the shop, waiting for an oil change. He went up to Jerry to watch the repair Jerry was making to an engine.

"It must be fun to work on airplanes," the man said.

"It sure is. I love it," replied Jerry.

"What's your hometown? You don't sound like a Floridian."

"Rochester, New York," Jerry answered.

For the Love of an Airplane

"Wow, Rochester. It seems like a lot of people ending up in Florida started out in the cold. I'm from a tiny place you probably don't know. It's one of those places where you can't get there from here, you know what I mean?"

"In New York?"

"Yes, it's a rural town in western New York called Wellsville."

"Of course! I know Wellsville like the back of my hand. I flew down there all the time."

"Really?"

"Yes." Jerry put his wrench down and turned to the man. "Let me tell you a story about Wellsville." Jerry recounted the story about the barn and buzzing the house.

"Oh, for heaven's sake. I don't believe it. You're the pilot who woke Mrs. Irving up from her nap to save the horses? She tells that story over and over and people don't believe her. A small airplane buzzing your house? Come on now. Gosh, I can't wait to tell her I actually met you! Hi, I'm Herbert," he said, reaching out and shaking Jerry's oily hand.

Jerry handed Herbert a rag. "Sorry, I got oil on you. Yes, I was giving a flight to my photographer friend, and he got several good pictures of the barn."

Herbert stood there wagging his head from side to side. "Amazing."

"Man must rise above the Earth—to the top of the atmosphere and beyond—for only thus will he fully understand the world in which he lives."
~Socrates

Chapter 13

Mustang P-51

Jerry entered the airport flight office building. Down a short hallway in the back, there was a pilot lounge. It sounds fancy, but it was just a small room with two thread-bare couches that that the airport manager has been unable to give away. A few navigation charts hung on the wall, and a coffee machine sat in the corner. It was always on and produced throat-burning brew tasting like yesterday's socks.

Jerry went over to the table and poured out a cup of the steaming coffee. "Does anyone know when this thing was last cleaned? It smells nasty."

Two of Jerry's airport friends ignored his rhetorical question, absorbed with the newspaper on the counter. Jerry looked over at Scott and Ben, who were looking at Trade-a-Plane. They were pointing to a North American Mustang P-51 for sale on the front page.

"Wow, would this be a dream to fly?" said Ben.

"Ahh." Scott sighed. "Yeah right. Lots of power here. A liquid-cooled, 12-cylinder, two-speed, two-stage-supercharged engine that produces 1,490 horsepower at sea level and 1,620 horsepower at 22,000 feet. Look at these specs."

"Jerry, what do you think of this?" Ben held up the newspaper and pointed to the Mustang. "Four-hundred MPH cruise. Can you imagine? Here's an idea. The Mustang is selling for $1,570. Two of us have Cubs, and along with Scott's Taylorcraft, we could all sell our airplanes and go in on this P-51 together."

Ben and Scott looked at Jerry. Jerry was the logical one in the group; his friends sought him out for advice.

"Let me look," Jerry said, picking up Trade-a-Plane. "You know there's an Army Air Force guy here on the field with one of these. When I joined the National Guard, I met him. Should we ask him about whether this is a good idea? Maybe find out about maintenance costs?"

"Fuel cost. That's what we need to find out," said Scott.

"You're right. Both," said Jerry.

"This is a great idea." Ben said. "Let's go find that guy. I know who you mean. Roger, I think, is his name."

Several hours later, the three men were in a hangar across the field, looking at Roger's P-51.

"So, we're thinking of going in on one of these," said Scott. "But we need to find out more about operating costs. How about fuel? How much does this burn?"

Roger looked at the three young men. "It's not bad. At cruise, it burns 85 gallons an hour; at economy cruise, it really sips at 60 gallons an hour."

The three men looked at each other, astonished. "Eighty-five gallons an hour? At 32 cents a gallon ... that's $27 an hour," Ben said, his mouth hanging open.

"That's my weekly salary at the maintenance shop," said Jerry.

"And almost $80 just to fill all the tanks. My entire flying Cub was only $320," said Ben.

"Not to mention other required maintenance plus oil ... oh gosh, I had no idea," said Jerry.

"And I thought the Continental 65-horse on the Cub was expensive at $1.40 an hour," said Scott.

The men all laughed.

Jerry looked at the Mustang and shook his head. "Well, looks like we're not going to buy a P-51 any time soon. Heck, you can't even take your girlfriend for a ride, it's single seat."

"She can go in your lap," said Scott.

They all laughed again and left Roger's hangar. Roger watched them go with a smile on his face. *Young impetuous pilots.*

Mustang P-51D

"It is not because things are difficult that we do not dare; it is because we do not dare that they are difficult."
~Seneca

Chapter 14

Sky King

Jerry turned 19. That week at the airport, a twin Cessna—a T-50, dubbed the "Bamboo Bomber" from the military UC-78B—the same type of airplane used to film *Sky King*, came in for an annual inspection. Seeing the airplane made Jerry think about how he needed some multi-engine time to get his next rating. Renting a twin was expensive; more than his weekly salary at the shop.

Eddie, the mechanic doing the inspection, was looking at the airplane as Jerry came into the hangar. He was explaining a repair to the owner.

"Look, you can see the entire left-wing fabric is bad," said Eddie.

For the Love of an Airplane

The owner had a dour expression on his face. "What's it going to cost to fix this?"

"I don't think you want to know. More than the airplane is worth, I'm afraid. Everything needs work, not just this wing. Little details."

Jerry tuned out as he looked the aircraft over. *A twin. This is what I need. Two Jacobs R-755-9s of 245 horsepower each. I wonder what fuel will cost. Let's see ...* he did the math in his head. *Twenty-five gallons an hour ... thirty-four cents per gallon ... $8.50 an hour. Glad I finally graduated math class.*

"Okay, well, never mind. I can't afford it. Can you sell it?" asked the owner.

"Are you sure?" asked Eddie.

"Yes, this thing is killing my finances. I'm going to have to give it up."

"There's a problem."

"What?"

"To sell it, we have to fix it."

"Okay, forget it. You can have it then."

Eddie parked the T-50 with the other derelicts in the field. Junk airplanes were everywhere.

How am I going to get that airplane? thought Jerry. He kept looking over at the twin while he was working every day. It didn't look that bad. After about a month, with the Cessna becoming more and more ragged, Jerry went to Eddie.

"Can I take that Cessna home?"

"Are you crazy? That beautiful cobwebbed rust bucket twin?"

They laughed.

"If you're serious, you can have it for $300."

"Where am I going to find $300?"

"Yeah, right, I know you. You have it saved up somewhere."

"Okay."

The next week Jerry started work recovering the left wing of the twin and going over all the details. After several months of work in his spare time, he had the old airplane running. Now he had the airplane for his multi-engine practice. He got his multi-engine rating just before turning 20, the same year he finally got his driver's license.

"Nothing is more expensive than a missed opportunity."
~H. Jackson Brown, Jr.

Chapter 15

Five Wacos

It was a beautiful spring day in Rochester. The air had a fresh smell as it rustled through the fields of new wildflower growth. The last dirt encrusted piles of winter snow had melted into puddles at the airport. Jerry decided to get some flying in.

He took off to the east in his Cub. He zipped up his jacket as the air turned cold through the vents. He decided to fly to little Cicero airport, outside of Syracuse. It was an easy flight of less than an hour. He'd been there once before.

He landed to the west and taxied up to the FBO hangar. Outside the building were five aircraft fuselages lined up next to each other. To Jerry, they appeared to be 1930 or 1931 Waco model RNFs. Intrigued, Jerry tied the Cub down and went into the hangar.

For the Love of an Airplane

Inside were engines for the Wacos in a neat row. The wings were all hanging up, along with the flying wires. Jerry couldn't believe what he was seeing. To even have one complete set of Waco RNF parts would be fantastic; that five sets of parts were sitting there just amazed him. They were probably super expensive because the condition looked so good. In fact, they looked new.

The airport manager came out of his office when he saw Jerry. "Hey kid, those are pretty nice, aren't they?" He pointed to the engines and wings.

"Yeah! I'll say they are." Jerry walked over to the manager and shook hands. "I'm Jerry."

"I'm Stan. These airplanes have been junked. You want 'em?"

"Junked? Yes sir, I sure do!" The words just rolled out of his mouth. Jerry couldn't help it. How could he say no to something like this? How he would get them to his house, he had no idea, but he would figure something out. Excitement flowed through him.

"Fifty bucks takes it all."

"Fifty bucks, great, yeah. Good deal. Okay!" Once again, the words rolled out of Jerry's mouth, but he knew he'd just spent $300 on the twin Cessna, leaving him about $5 to his name.

"Ah, I'll need to gather the money and come back."

"Okay, that's fine. Here's my phone number. See you when you get back." Stan handed Jerry a piece of paper with a number scrawled on it, with the words "Five Wacos - Stanley."

Jerry put the paper in his pocket. He wandered among the engines and wings, feeling ecstatic. *Warner Scarab radials with 110 horsepower each.* He kneeled in front of one engine, looking at the casing and cylinders, inhaling the wonderful smells of the machinery. *This is great. Am I dreaming? Gotta be.*

With a smile and a light step, he left the hangar and got back in the Cub. He took one more look at the fuselages. *Perfect. He would rebuild every single one. He could probably sell a flying RNF for $150.*

It was all he could think about for the rest of the weekend. How was he going to come up with the money? Reality set in as he realized he was going to have to figure out a way to get the $50.

The next day, he was back in school. He got up the nerve to discuss the problem with Mr. Wood. He waited after class for the students around Mr. Wood to disperse.

"Mr. Wood. I have a dilemma. I need your advice."

"Of course." Mr. Wood turned to Jerry with his full attention.

Jerry explained his visit to Cicero and detailed the condition of the Wacos. Mr. Wood listened patiently. He knew Jerry to be thorough and conscientious, so he knew he wasn't making anything up.

"But, you know, I bought the Cessna to take my lessons in, and have about $2 left," said Jerry, with a concerned look on his face.

Mr. Wood pursed his lips and was quiet for a moment. "I can loan you $25. You can pay it back as you get it. I trust you."

Jerry was surprised and delighted. "Thank you, Mr. Wood, thank you! I'll find the other half somehow."

For the Love of an Airplane

Jerry knew that the $25 Mr. Wood was giving him was half of his weekly salary.

That night, Jerry tossed and turned. Where was he going to get the other $25? At the airport that day, he'd asked if he could get an advance on salary. Old Stopplebeiner said absolutely not. He wracked his brain for a solution. He had a truck and a willing driver; he had a place to store the airplanes, but he needed $25.

The next day, Mr. Wood came up to him. "Any luck?"

"Nope. None. I figure, you know, if you go to the store for shoes and you don't have the money to buy the shoes, then you can't have the shoes."

"I understand. Well, some day this will work out in a different way, that's my philosophy in life. When you try to do the right thing, at some point you're rewarded," said Mr. Wood.

"I hope you're right. Here's your $25 back." Jerry handed Mr. Wood the cash he'd given him, crestfallen.

About six weeks later, summer was in full bloom. Jerry flew back to Cicero. The image of the five Wacos had been printed into his memory. He taxied over to the hangar, noticing that the fuselages were gone. *Someone bought them for big bucks*, he thought.

The manager came out of the office as Jerry entered the hangar. The parts that had been lined up, along with the engines, were all gone.

"Hey kid! Where the hell were you?"

"Yeah, Stan. I'm so sorry, I couldn't get the money."

"I gave you my phone number! Why didn't you call me?"

"I couldn't get the money Stan, I couldn't get the money."

"Jeez, kid, if you would have called me, I would have given them to you. I hired a junk dealer to haul them off. I was going to give them to you, and you don't show up and no call."

Jerry's jaw dropped open, and he felt a rock form in his stomach. The world had turned on one end. He began to breathe heavily. He shut his eyes, hoping he was dreaming, and he'd wake from the nightmare screaming.

"Oh, no!" A bead of sweat ran down Jerry's forehead as he tried to catch his breath.

Stan looked at him and shook his head. "Hey Kid. I'm sorry for you. But let this be a lesson. Never take the first number, okay, and let people know what's going on. I figured you'd say $25 or something and then I'd surprise you and say just come get 'em."

"I feel like an idiot. I'm sorry, Stan. I am so sorry."

"Nothing to be done about it now. Dammit, I wish you'd called me."

Jerry walked out of the hangar, dejected and disappointed. He was mad at himself. He had done it to himself. Why didn't he call Stan? *Because I was afraid to call. Because I was shy. Because I didn't have the money.*

When Jerry got back to school on Monday, he recounted the story to Mr. Wood and two of his classmates. They were shocked and astonished as he described what Stan had told him about the five Wacos.

"So, do you think I could have called Stan and asked for one airplane for the $25? Or two airplanes? What a dumb jerk I was. I can't believe it. I just can't believe it."

"Jeez. Can you imagine that, if you'd gotten five Waco RNFs? I can't believe it either," said Henry.

"I'm sick about it," said Jerry.

"Well, it sure sounds like he gave you some good advice. I bet you'll never forget it," said Ben.

"No, I won't."

"Life's like that, guys, you have to roll with the tides," said Mr. Wood. "You guys are young; there's still plenty of learning and lessons that will come your way. If you can learn something from each calamity, then you're smart."

Mr. Wood paused a moment and then went on. "Speaking of rolling, I have bad news and good news for you. The bad news is that the aviation class is being suspended this year, right after you guys graduate."

"Why?"

"Because the aviation jobs have dropped off here in Rochester and it doesn't make sense to keep holding the class with only a few people interested."

"Well, I'm sure glad we got through it first," said Henry.

"If that's the bad news, what's the good news?" asked Ben.

"The good news is that we're giving away the airplanes we've been working on in class. There'll be plenty of junk for you all to pick what you want. Jerry, how would you like the Waco RNF?"

"Yes!"

Jerry is first from the left

"There is only one corner of the universe you can be certain of improving, and that's your own self."
~Aldous Huxley

Chapter 16

Florida

Brother Bill and Jerry were sitting on the porch at Bill and Jack's in the islands. The summer was almost over; they could feel the change in the air. The afternoon wind rippled the water on the lake in front of them. Jerry and Bill had just gotten back from a little fishing. Jerry leaned back in the old Adirondack chair and sighed.

"I wish Dad was alive to see me graduate from high school. I don't think Mom or Dad thought I could do that. And then remember me telling you that Mom chewed me out for saying I was going to own and fly an airplane some day? I did it!"

"He was proud of you, Jer. And I know Mom is, said Bill.

"You wouldn't know it."

For the Love of an Airplane

"That's how she is. Have you decided if you're going to go to college?"

"I don't know. Can you take aviation in college?"

"I'm not sure. It's not very common; it's not like becoming an engineer or a doctor, but if you wanted to manage an airport, I imagine it would be helpful."

"It doesn't matter as long as it's aviation."

"The question is, what do you love? You've had plenty of exposure to piloting and working on airplanes. What do you want to do all day?"

"I'll start with mechanics. I love it. The question is, can I make a living doing that?"

"You know, there's an aircraft technician school near my apartment in Miami. Come down and stay with me. I did a little digging and found out that in 1925, two guys—T. Higbee Embry and John Paul Riddle—one an entrepreneur and one a barnstormer—launched the Embry-Riddle Company, which became the Embry-Riddle International School of Aviation and then Embry-Riddle Aeronautical Institute. They located in Miami, and trained pilots and mechanics for World War II. It's probably the best flight and mechanic training facility anywhere in the world. They even had a seaplane base with an all-female division during the war."

"No kidding? That's something. Thanks Bill. I'll think about that. I'm tired of the cold up here in the winter, anyway. Florida sounds great."

"Flying is learning how to throw yourself at the ground and miss."
~ Douglas Adams

Chapter 17

1958: Banners

After graduating high school, Jerry continued to work full time at the Rochester airport. After he got his multi-engine rating in the Cessna, he obtained an instrument rating and his certified instructor (CFI) rating.

He spent his spare time rebuilding the derelicts strewn through the fields around the airport. He was the go-to person if machinery wasn't working. As a pilot, he was smooth and competent, with a sixth sense for the operation of the controls. This made him a sought-out instructor. He wasn't just building time, like many of the flight instructors were trying to do to get into the airlines; he simply loved teaching people how to fly.

After doing the research on the aviation school his brother recommended—Embry-Riddle—he decided it made sense.

For the Love of an Airplane

There was nothing holding him in Rochester except for family, and he could visit them just like Bill did.

The Embry-Riddle program was 18 months. Jerry couldn't leave Rochester until he had the money for tuition. He planned and saved. He rebuilt the Cub and sold it. He sold the Cessna Twin. Then he bought a 1954 Plymouth so he could get around Miami. He drove to Florida and enrolled in Embry-Riddle.

Instead of dorms, the college had room rentals and apartments next door. Many of the students were cash poor, just like Jerry, so five guys rented one room with five beds in it. They missed a lot of meals and learned to show up at the guys' parents' houses just before dinnertime.

Jerry got straight A's in all of his aviation subjects at Embry-Riddle. When he graduated, he went to work at North Perry Airport maintaining the flight instruction aircraft fleet. He could fly the airplanes anytime he wanted, so he got plenty of hours in. He took odd jobs, like banner towing, and some carpentry projects. Not only was he a natural at aircraft mechanics, he had a talent for woodworking. Structure simply made sense to him and he found it all easy to master. He continued to be the go-to guy for the other mechanics in troubleshooting aircraft and diagnosing engine and performance ailments.

One day, he was at the airport doing an engine replacement. The banner towers were at work, picking up the advertising signs with small airplanes and then flying down the beach nearby. Jerry had learned how to pick up and drop a tow; it looked simple from the ground but it was a technique that could turn into an accident if you weren't careful. A special grappling hook was attached to the plane. The pilot would lower the hook to snag a rope connected to the banner laid out on the ground. The pilot would then climb out with the banner behind, a tricky maneuver that required impeccable timing with experienced and precise actions from the pilot. They used small biplanes for the tows, since it looked cool to the audiences on the beach. People always look at biplanes.

Jerry watched as his friend Thomas dropped a tow with a 1929 BIRD, a small biplane with a Continental radial engine. Thomas landed and headed for the gas pump. After fueling, he hand-propped the plane to get it going again.

The BIRD would have none of it. Thomas wore himself out trying to get the airplane to start. Two mechanics near Jerry went out and gave it a try. Nothing. Jerry put down his wrench and wiped his hands with a rag. Then he went over to the airplane.

"Jeez, I'll lose money on this if I can't run this last banner this afternoon," said Thomas.

"Well, let me have a turn," said Jerry.

"Good luck."

Since his near-death-by-prop experience when he was a line boy, uninformed on how to perform the prop start safely, Jerry had started hundreds of aircraft. He thought nothing of it now, but was also fully aware of the danger.

He put his hands flat on the left blade and pulled it down. He expected a start. Nothing. He tried again. Nothing. Three more tries and he was tiring. Sometimes he wondered if God was teasing him.

"Thomas, are you positive the switch is on? You might have an electrical problem."

"It's on, it's on," said Thomas.

"Okay, let me try again." *Come on, come on. One more. Probably a wire open.*

He threw himself into the pull. As he did, the gravel moved under his shoes, sliding. The engine started, and the prop was turning in a blur. The combination of loose gravel and slippery footing propelled him toward the airplane. Jerry fell straight into the rotating propeller. Instinctively, his arm went out to the spinner to keep the rest of his body from moving into it. He made contact with the spinning hub with the palm of his right hand. He pushed off the hub like his life depended on it, which it did, the metal twisting in his hand. He fell backwards into the gravel and rolled as fast as he could to the left to get clear of the spinning prop.

The mechanics and bystanders were gasping and shouting expletives as the event took all of five seconds. As Jerry rolled away from the front of the airplane, a collective sigh of relief came from the crowd. Jerry sat there, stunned. He moved his head from side to side.

"Oh, my God." He looked at the palm of his hand. It was red and bruised, but not bleeding. *I am some lucky sonofabitch.*

Thomas waved and taxied off to pick up his afternoon tow like nothing had happened.

Sometimes Jerry felt like life was trying to kill him.

"Life is not about waiting for the storm to pass but learning to dance in the rain."
~Vivian Greene

Chapter 18

1959: Interruptions

Jerry moved to Executive Airport in Fort Lauderdale, going to work for Riley Aeronautics. Riley had just constructed a maintenance hangar at the airport. The area was about to get very busy, as tenants were discovering lower rental prices and moving up from Miami.

Jerry worked on Cessna 310 modifications for Riley. The mods were so performance-enhancing, they called them Riley Rockets. The Riley Rocket 310 and the Riley Turbostream 310 replaced the standard Continental 310 hp engines with Lycoming TIO-540 350 hp engines. These turbocharged intercooled engines were installed with three-blade Hartzell propellers in a counter-rotating configuration to further increase performance and single-engine safety.

The modifications required detailed mechanical and electrical work. Jerry loved it. He also liked his boss, Jack, who immediately identified Jerry's dedication and ability. Riley was a creative thinker with a good sense for business and marketing.

One day, Jerry was feeling sick and went to talk to Jack Riley.

"Do what you need to do," said Jack. "We'll be here when you get back."

It was rare for any illness or injury to keep Jerry from working on airplanes.

When he got home, he tumbled into bed, feeling like he had an infection of some kind. He noticed that his left testicle had ballooned into a painful mass. He decided to rest and wait for the infection to clear.

I might need to go to the doctor for antibiotics. I don't really want to. Cindy will tell me I have to go.

The next day, he woke up in excruciating pain.

"Stop groaning!"

"I can't help it."

"Go to the doctor," said Cindy. "That's more than an infection."

Cindy was a nurse. Jerry knew she was right. *But nurses were so bossy.*

In the waiting room, Jerry started feeling worse. The doctor's nurse noticed and called him into the office ahead of the other patients. Dr. Kirk walked in. He performed an exam, and they took blood for testing. Then they x-rayed the testicle.

Dr. Kirk flipped on the viewer and loaded the image. "Look at this. It's a mass," said Dr. Kirk. "I don't like the looks of it at all. I'm going to numb it up and stick a needle in for a biopsy."

"Oh great," Jerry said.

"I'm glad you haven't lost your sense of humor," replied Dr. Kirk.

After the procedure, he was given antibiotics and pain pills and told to return the next day. He got home, barely able to walk. Cindy looked at him and shook her head.

"You're a sad case. Quit your bellyaching. Didn't he give you anything for pain?"

"It hasn't worked yet."

Nurses sure are a rough bunch. I guess they have to be. But why did I marry one?

The next day, he was back at the doctor's office after calling to tell Mr. Riley of his predicament. They took him straight in. Dr. Kirk came in with a clipboard with test results. He slid the x-ray image up into the viewer again.

"Look." He pointed to the upper right portion of the mass with his pen.

"It doesn't look good," replied Jerry.

"It's not. It's cancer."

"Jesus Christ. I'm only 23."

Dr. Kirk was quiet a moment. Then he took a deep breath. "The day after tomorrow, show up at the hospital at noon. We'll prep you and do surgery the following morning. The whole testicle is coming off. Then you'll have three months of cobalt radiation."

For the Love of an Airplane

"What about, ah, what about …."

"What about function? Don't worry. You still have the other one. You'll be fine. Why do you think you have two?" Dr. Kirk smiled and placed his hand on Jerry's shoulder.

They both laughed.

"Good. I finally got you to laugh," said Dr. Kirk.

When Jerry got home, he didn't even hear Cindy yelling at him.

"When we long for life without difficulties, remind us that oaks grow strong in contrary winds and diamonds are made under pressure."
~ Peter Marshall

Chapter 19

Butternut Squash

In the three months following the surgery, Jerry got sicker and sicker. The cobalt radiation was agonizing for him. Once a healthy 155 pounds, he dropped to 96 pounds. An already lanky five foot nine, he now looked like he was going to expire any day. He couldn't catch his breath; he walked haltingly, like an old man. He could eat Jello and drink some milk. He was nauseous most of the time.

Despite his sickness, Jerry continued to show up at the airport to work. Riley really liked Jerry, admired his spunk and his ethics, and decided to keep him working so he could collect his paycheck.

"Brian, don't tell Jerry you're checking his work. He'd be insulted. But please go along after him and make sure he gets everything right. I know he's making mistakes; he's halfway delirious," said Riley to his shop manager. "I really like the young man. He's sharper than my best guys, even on his worst days."

"Will do."

Without realizing it, Jerry made an assortment of mistakes. One of his jobs was to install the fuel pumps on to the modified engines. As Jerry finished each job, Brian came behind him to make corrections. Some were fine; others weren't.

It was the third week after stopping the three months of cobalt treatment that Jerry felt life coming back. Cindy put a bowl of butternut squash in front of him with a dollop of brown sugar and a square of butter on top. Jerry devoured the squash and then took a deep breath. "Wow."

Continuing this emotional account of the ordeal, Jerry pauses. He goes on:

"I have to add this. About twenty years later, I was in the restaurant at Executive Airport called SkyTel. The place was very popular for lunch, and it was packed that day. My business then was on Exec and I went over to SkyTel once in a while. It had a great view of the runway. When I walked in, there was one table left. I was sitting there eating lunch and there was one chair across from me. I saw this guy walk in and he's looking around and there wasn't anything available. I motioned him to come over and sit with me.

We got talking about Executive Airport and how it had changed over the years. I told him I had worked for Riley.

He says, 'Yeah, I remember Riley. I'm an MD. I have a practice in the area. I was taking flight lessons at Riley in the late fifties. There was this very young man who worked for Riley as a mechanic and he had cancer. I was in medical training, so it sort of struck me. We all were really worried about him. You were working for Riley then. Any idea of what happened to the guy?'

I looked at this doctor and nodded. I held my hand up. 'I do know the man. You're looking at him.'

He looked at me with astonishment. He grabbed my hand and he almost shook my arm off.

'I'm so happy to see you! I can't believe that you survived that. What a time! Oh my goodness, I can't believe it. You weighed less than a hundred pounds. We didn't think you'd make it. What a wonderful day this is!'

You know, like that being the only chair available in the restaurant and him coming in at that time, and me being at a table without being with somebody else, what a coincidence. It was great. It was really great."

"To open a business is very easy; to keep it open is very difficult."
~Chinese proverb

Chapter 20

The Lure of a Business

From the moment Jerry dragged the PT-26 derelict home, he thought about running his own shop. While most of the mechanics he'd worked with were more than happy to take orders and directions from others, Jerry was always seeing things that were missed or not optimized. He knew that if he got to call the shots, things would be right. He also knew that maintenance was a money game. Everyone had to make something. He knew that his design for maintenance and repair, including rebuilding, could be re-ordered and organized so that efficiencies were built in. It had always been obvious to him, but he never found a boss who could think far enough ahead in arranging the work.

Starting a business, however, was complicated. Every time he'd think of it, he realized all the entanglements of hiring staff and maintaining the location. Then he'd get discouraged and go back to single-handed, one-at-a-time restorations. The work kept coming in, and he had a waiting list.

Jerry says, "In the 1970s, work started to dry up as the recession hit. I maintained a Cessna 150 for a superintendent working construction. One day he said, 'Jerry. You've got an eye for structure and for design. You'd make a good layout man.'

"I ended up working construction and continued to repair and recover aircraft on the weekends. At one outfit I joined, we built several thousand homes. As the superintendent, I handled 300 homes at a shot. The whole time I was building homes, though, I thought about airplanes. But I learned a lot about construction and realized that the way I'd manage a construction company would be the way I'd run an aircraft restoration company. To me, it was a formula; plan, communicate, execute.

"When I left that company, I got my general contractor's license and started Florida Sunshine Builders. We built high end custom homes. At that time—1970s and 1980s—sales were booming in South Florida. A side benefit was building my own home, one at a time, and then selling it for twice what I invested a few years later. It was a great business to be in because it didn't take much infrastructure to maintain. You just had to understand what needed to be done and how to translate that for subcontractors. There was one problem: I missed the airplanes. I'd wake up in the mornings and think, *if only I were going to the airport*.

"After putting in long days building custom homes, I'd go to the airport. *If I were single, I would live at the airport*, I thought. As much as I made a good living in construction, the oxygen was always at the airport. The plan kept playing out in my mind. How could I do what I love full time?"

Jerry works on the engines for the Grumman Goose

Grumman Goose National Air and Space Museum 2002

For the Love of an Airplane

"The air up there in the clouds is very pure and fine, bracing and delicious. And why shouldn't it be? It is the same the angels breathe."
~Mark Twain

Chapter 21

The Birth of BIPE

Jerry recounts his early business days.

"I knew I wanted to work on, and fly, airplanes. But like every other young person out there intent on a career, the job you love may not be the job that puts food on the table. I wrestled with this for a long time. I always want to see a level of quality that takes time. Getting things exactly right was, and is, more important than making money. This has been the thorniest issue throughout my career; how do I make enough to not worry about the bills? This was one reason I went into residential construction. I figured I could save the money and then work on airplanes on the weekends.

"Then it hit me. I'd been taking airplane junk and rebuilding it for myself; then I'd sell it and make a profit. With the money saved, I could pay for school, buy a car, and fund the other things. The projects I was working on were done to my own specifications, what I wanted the airplane to be. Why not flip this upside down and ask the customer what they wanted before even stating a project? When the customer wants a restoration, or a new cover job, they have a level of expectation that I felt I could fulfill. I could do that at the same time I asked the customer what kind of paint scheme did they want; what customizations might they want, and I could explain all the things we could do to make their airplane their dream aircraft. If I had a few customers with that situation, I could start and stay in business. The customer would make the investment, and I would execute on the plan.

"I was thinking about this one day as I was building a Stearman. A guy who lived near the airport stopped by to chat. His name was Walt. He kept looking at what I was doing.

'That Stearman is going to be beautiful,' said Walt. 'You know, Jerry, I have a dream for an airplane I've always wanted.'

'What airplane?'

'A Tiger Moth,' Walt said.

'Ah, a de Havilland DH.82 Tiger Moth. A 1930s British biplane designed by Geoffrey de Havilland and built by the de Havilland Aircraft Company. It has a de Havilland Gipsy Major engine in it, an inverted, four-cylinder, air-cooled arrangement with 130 horsepower. Okay. Let's find one in pieces somewhere. You buy it and bring it here and I'll restore it.'

"Walt had a gleam in his eye, smiling. 'I hadn't thought of that.'

"We each looked at the other and nodded. Walt left, excited and intent on fulfilling his dream.

"He quickly found several possibilities, and I checked them out for him. I ended up doing the Tiger Moth; Walt was delighted, and BIPE was up and running. I picked BIPE as a name because it's logical. BIPE stands for BIPLANE. TRIPE, for example, stands for TRIPLANE. It says it all.

"I had a ton of fabric covering work come my way after that. People saw my Stearman, and they saw the Tiger Moth, and apparently no one else knew how to cover a tube and fabric aircraft. In fact, come to think of it, there aren't a lot of places now, as I relate this in 2024, that do show-plane-type fabric work.

"At the time, Sam Lyons, the famous painter of all things aviation, saw my Stearman and asked me if he could paint it. Of course I said yes. It ended up being one of his best sellers. It's called *Airshow*.

For the Love of an Airplane

I was hanging out in Sam's booth at the Sun-n-Fun airshow in Lakeland, Florida, after he painted my Stearman. A young woman came into the booth and saw the t-shirt with *Airshow* on it. She loved it and asked Sam to sign the shirt after buying it. I stood in the corner, watching. Once Sam finished signing it, with the girl beaming, I walked over and picked up the shirt and the sharpie. The girl backed up a step in surprise and confusion. I laid the shirt carefully back out on the counter and signed the corner across from Sam's signature. The young girl's elation and surprise turned to upset, and she rocked from foot to foot, not sure what to say.

'What's your name?' I asked the girl.

'Sarah.'

'Sarah, you are now the only person in the world with an *Airshow* t-shirt that is signed by the artist, *and* the builder and owner of the aircraft.'

"Sarah switched from being confused and angry to being ecstatic, hugging me and Sam alternately and jumping up and down. I've never seen anyone that excited."

"Coincidence is God's way of remaining anonymous."
~Albert Einstein

Chapter 22

1999: A Chance Meeting

Jerry located BIPE INC at the Executive Airport in Fort Lauderdale, Florida. He'd been working out of a single T-hangar for years, figuring out how to move things around and make the most of the space for restoration work. But it was tight. He rented the hangar next to his; if he could work on two airplanes at once, it would pay for itself. Executive airport was getting busier and busier.

The tiny "business office" at eight by twelve feet in size was just big enough for a desk, a small couch, and a chair. But it was air-conditioned. In Florida, that was a welcome upgrade. When Jerry would finish spray coatings on aircraft surfaces, he'd walk from 98 degrees into 68 degrees and collapse in the office chair. Jerry's airport buddies quickly learned that in the Florida summers, the place to hang out was Jerry's office. That is, if you could fit inside. Air conditioning was still a luxury in the hangar offices. Jerry happened to be in his "air-conditioned executive suite" when Ron Alexander called.

"Jerry, I lost one of my instructors last minute because of illness. I have a workshop coming up in Lakeland this weekend. Can you drop everything and come teach fabric?"

"Absolutely."

Ron sighed in relief. "I knew it. You're so dependable."

"Well, I have more free time now, Ron. I just divorced."

"Jerry! I'm sorry! Do you want me to find another instructor? Are you okay?"

"I'm okay Ron, I'm okay. It's been building for a long time. Being at the airport, and teaching, are therapeutic for me."

"Okay, good. I'm looking forward to seeing you. We'll talk."

Lakeland was less than a four-hour drive from Fort Lauderdale. Jerry looked forward to teaching. Ron had made it so smooth for him, easing the awkward moments at the beginning and showing him it was simply sharing knowledge with students. Now he looked forward to the classes. He remembered how hard it had been to get up in front of a class in school. Here he was, getting ready to spend two days in front of students.

The workshops were on the weekend so that working adults could attend. The model worked well; the classes were in a huge hangar where they could literally fit four workshops into the four corners of the commercial hangar. The workshops were hands on, with the opportunity to practice and make mistakes before going home to work on an airplane.

Each class had materials, textbooks, a whiteboard, and seating. Instructors would show up early and do the set-up and arrange things the way they wanted. Saturday morning, Jerry had just finished his setup when Ron came over to him with a student in tow.

"Jerry, I want to introduce you to a customer and a friend. Lisa Turner has already built a Pulsar XP, and she's now about to build a fabric covered KOLB Mark III. Lisa, meet Jerry. He restores airplanes and knows more about fabric than the fabric people do. I think highly of both of you, and wanted to make the introduction before class."

Lisa and Jerry looked each other in the eye and shook hands with a firm shake and a smile.

"Thanks Ron," said Jerry.

"I'm looking forward to learning about fabric," said Lisa. "The Pulsar was all metal, wood, and fiberglass; the KOLB is tube and fabric, so I need to find out how to do it right before I screw anything up."

"We'll definitely give you the opportunity to screw up here," said Jerry.

All three laughed. Ron left to check on the other instructors and setups.

Lisa turned back to Jerry. "One question I have is about painting. I didn't paint my Pulsar; I was scared to death of ruining it. After all that work, to not have it look professional concerned me. But if I'm going to keep building airplanes, I should learn how to paint them."

"Hmm, we need to get you some painting practice," said Jerry. "Are you from around here?"

"Boynton Beach, Florida."

"Well, that's great. I'm in Fort Lauderdale. That's a 45-minute drive. I'll show you how to paint, if you'd like."

"That would be perfect," replied Lisa.

The next weekend, they spent time applying fabric and coatings at Jerry's shop at Exec. Lisa laughed when he showed her the "executive suite" office.

"At least it's air-conditioned," commented Lisa.

"All the space here is pretty cramped," said Jerry.

"What you need is your own large hangar," said Lisa.

"That's a dream I've had for a long time," said Jerry.

One day Jerry and Lisa were at the Lantana airport, close to Lisa's house. Lantana airport was a rustic, non-towered airport nestled in the outer ring of Palm Beach airspace. With three long runways, it was a pilot's dream. Lisa wanted to show him where she had taken her flight lessons. They wandered around the busy little airport and then went into the main office. They saw an ad for a hangar. The hangar was at the end of a row of T-hangars, faced the field, and was large enough for four aircraft.

"I just got an idea," said Jerry. He looked at Lisa.

"I know what you're thinking."

"Yeah?"

"Yeah. You could save a lot of money if you move up here and operate out of this for-sale hangar."

"You're right; that's exactly what I was thinking."

Lantana Airport (LNA)

Jerry moved his operation to Lantana in 2001. He built a second floor into the space, giving them a full-sized office and restroom facilities, as well as an air-conditioned work room. It was heaven to Jerry, and nostalgic for Lisa, who had kept her Pulsar aircraft in the hangar next to it.

For the Love of an Airplane

Jerry decided to take on full-time employees. He knew it would be a challenge because of the training necessary, but with a long waiting list of customers, it was time to test his business blueprint.

Jerry interviewed candidates. He explained to each of them what an apprenticeship meant, telling them they would be paid a low wage but given on-the-job training. While he couldn't force them to stay, he hoped that if they accepted the position, they would give him at least two years of service.

In return, they would receive invaluable training in fabric covering, mechanics, the use of tools, safety practices, painting, and woodworking. Most of the candidates were just out of school, since they could afford to take the time. The other category where he found apprentices was in the job-retired group. In fact, these folks ended up not caring about the pay, and adored the work.

Lantana Crew

As Jerry juggled the demand for services with the need for good employees, he realized that the balance between income and expenses was delicate. Payroll, taxes, benefits, and the cost of training were all high.

In 2007, the costs had gone up so much for the location that Jerry thought about relocating. At the same time, Lisa was caught up in a major restructuring. She was the Chief Training Officer for Tyco in Boca Raton, Florida. Most professional people view layoffs as a catastrophe, and Lisa was no different.

At home that night, Jerry and Lisa looked out over the postage stamp back yard and tiny lake where they lived in Boynton Beach. The palm trees were swaying, the breeze was gently rolling through the patio; the sunshine danced on the walls.

"What more would you want? Said Lisa. This is beautiful. After being laid off, maybe I'll just stay home and chill out."

"What more could you want? Well, for one, you can't land a seaplane in that little pond," he waved to the water, "and it's damn hot; and there aren't any mountains in the distance."

"Okay. Let's move. I'll look for seaplane-friendly lakes."

The next night, Lisa pulled out a map and pointed to a lake that straddled two states: North Carolina and Georgia. "Lake Chatuge. There's a nice little mountain town next to it called Hayesville."

Jerry said, "Let's go."

For the Love of an Airplane

"When fears are grounded, dreams take flight."
~Anon

Chapter 23

2008: Andrews, North Carolina

As the airport manager showed Jerry where the hangar could be built, Jerry had a "If you build it, they will come" moment. The manager pointed to a large plot of land across from a row of T-hangars.

"Put whatever you want there," said the manager.

It was a dream come true. *I can build a hangar exactly to my specifications*, he thought as he looked at the plot of land.

The next day, Jerry sketched out a plan. It included a large workroom and a spray paint booth; upstairs would be a large office, a storage room, and a classroom for training activities.

The building went up fast. Within six months, Jerry had the Certificate of Occupancy and a healthy long-term lease. "Okay, now the question is, will the business arrive?" he asked himself.

For the Love of an Airplane

By the time Jerry moved the last of the equipment up from Florida, the list had grown to five airplanes.

The hangar at KRHP

Back in Florida, the man who had started out working for BIPE as an apprentice five years earlier was now making his own waiting list of airplanes to come in for fabric covering.

The blueprint is working.

Soon after getting set up in Andrews, the phone rang.

"Jerry? This is Charles Park. I'm in Ohio and have some aircraft parts I want to get rid of. One of them is a 1941 UPF-7 Waco fuselage with wings and wires, and everything to assemble the

The crew at KRHP 2009

airplane together. I'm cleaning up the yard. My friend Bill here said you restore airplanes. Do you want it, or do you have a customer who wants it?

When Jerry heard the word "Waco," a tiny voice in his head activated, saying, "Waco? Don't make a mistake! Don't let opportunity pass you by!"

Jerry was about to say, "No thanks, but I'll check around." Instead, he said, "Can you send me some pictures?"

"Sure."

They exchanged email addresses, and then Jerry forgot about it. Later in the day, he got the pictures on email. "What do you make of this?" Jerry pulled up the pictures on the computer to show Lisa.

"Look at all the junk in that field! I see a tractor and a firetruck; where's the airplane?"

For the Love of an Airplane

"Here's the fuselage," Jerry pointed to the rusted frame in the foreground. "And there are the wings and wires over there by the tractor."

"Yikes. Is it a good deal?"

"It's a very good deal. A three-seat airplane with a Continental W670-6A, 7-cylinder radial engine that's in good condition, and a Hamilton Standard ground adjustable prop with polished blades."

"As in, five Wacos for $50 deal?" said Lisa with a smile.

They both laughed, recalling the heart-wrenching opportunity-lost story.

"Okay, I may have finally learned my lesson. I should consider this one. I'd have to go pick it up, though. If the deal is good enough, it could be worth it."

"What a mess. Does he have all the parts?" asked Lisa.

"He says he does, but I've never heard someone say that about any airplane and it actually have all the parts."

"It's your investment."

Lisa walked out of the office later, hearing Jerry on the phone. "Charles? When do you want me there?"

Jerry and Justin, one of the BIPE mechanics, made the drive to Ohio. Several days later, they pulled up in front of the hangar with a trailer full of rusted aircraft parts and began unloading them into a corner.

"This is an airplane?" asked Lisa.

"Ah, well, parts of an airplane," said Jerry. "There are a lot of parts missing."

"I was wondering about that."

1941 Waco UPF-7

"But it's the data tag that matters."

"Right, of course, nothing is legal without the registration."

Jerry explains this over and over to the people who call on the phone for free pre-buy advice. Jerry asks them to send pictures, and as he views them on email, he asks the question. "Does the airplane have a data tag and is it the same number that's on the registration?"

Half the time, the caller says, "What data tag?"

"Without the data tag and registration, you won't own the airplane," says Jerry.

On weekends, Jerry would head to the airport and work on the 1941 Waco UPF-7.

Several weeks after picking up the Waco, Jerry was in the workshop trying to organize the boxes and components for the airplane. As Lisa walked in, Jerry sat down on a chair next to the old rusted fuselage and sighed.

"This UPF-7 is confusing me right from the start. All these parts and pieces, no plans, and not even sure what set of plans I should be looking for on the internet."

"Better you than me. That's why I like the aircraft kits that give you all the parts and then tell you what to do with them."

"I've always wanted a UPF-7," Jerry said as he sorted through some rusted hardware. "But this project is going to be a test of my patience."

"You're the one, then. I don't know anyone with more patience than you. We need to name it. That should help."

"Okay. Pick a name."

"Hmm. An airplane name. Well, name it Kay. If you ever finish and sell it, it will be your 401K, as in savings account," said Lisa.

"Good, I like it. But I'll make it KayLee, since you're my girlfriend, your nickname is Lee, and guys name airplanes after their favorite women."

Lisa smiled. "Just don't put a picture of me in a bathing suit on the side of it."

The UPF-7 was not just a test of Jerry's patience, but also a test of BIPE's ability to make or obtain parts that were not available, and make the upgrades that Jerry had dreamed about, like metal fuel tank covers, custom switch panels, a good set of brakes, and a brilliant red color with silver and gold trim.

Since the Waco was Jerry's project, the customer's airplanes came first, and were worked on first on the schedule. On Sundays Jerry would disappear into the corner where the Waco was coming together. It was a mixture of therapy and frustration. But Jerry's hallmark is perseverance, so bit by bit the airplane came together.

One day Lisa went into the corner of the workshop where the Waco was coming together and sat down on a mechanic's creeper. Jerry was making notes and pondering how to make a part.

"Tell me what is special about this particular airplane," asked Lisa.

For the Love of an Airplane

Jerry put his notes down and looked at the fuselage.

"I've rebuilt dozens of Stearmans, Cubs, Taylorcraft, Aeronca, and other small airplanes, but less than a dozen Wacos. The Wacos are much more challenging. The plans may or may not be accurate, depending on what collection of parts you get, and some of the parts have to be made. But that challenge is exactly why I love the airplane. This particular UPF-7 model is a delight to fly."

In 2021, ten years later, KayLee made her first flight.

"That was the most challenging project I've done," Jerry commented, while looking at the finished airplane.

BIPE was hitting its stride as more people realized just what Jerry could accomplish.

Part Two: Medical Mysteries

"Only those who risk going too far can possibly find out how far one can go."
~T.S. Eliot

Chapter 24

A Longer Term of Service

The story of Jerry Stadtmiller would not be complete without the backdrop of health issues explained. That Jerry survived birth at 23 weeks old is itself a miracle and explains some of the other challenges.

After Jerry's cancer in 1959, his health was good. It wasn't until 2004, a year after he wedded Lisa Turner, that problems arose (we hope the two events are not connected). His general physician noticed circulation abnormalities, and sent him to a cardiologist. They did a stress test and found blockages. The cardiologist sent Jerry to the hospital, and the doctor's office called Lisa at work.

Arriving in the prep area, Lisa went over to Jerry. She looked down with a stern expression. "Look. We got married last year. I just want you to understand that you signed up for a longer term of service."

Everyone in the room laughed, even Jerry. "Okay. Tell that to the doctors," replied Jerry.

The cardiologist told Jerry he needed to have open-heart bypass surgery. Alternatively, and perhaps not as effective, he could get a few stents.

"How fast can I get back to work?" asked Jerry.

"You say you are a mechanic?"

"Yes."

"Two months with bypass, a week with stents."

"Stents," said Jerry.

They installed a few stents, and Jerry was back to work within two days.

The following year, Jerry was back at the cardiologist for a routine checkup.

"Looking good," said Dr. Evers. "But ...."

"But?" Jerry asked. "I hate it when doctors follow up with 'but.'"

"But the arteries in your legs are shutting down."

"Shutting down?"

"Narrowing. I want you to see a specialist."

"Okay."

The following week, Jerry and Lisa drove to the University of Miami to a vascular specialist.

"Do you have pain in the legs?" Dr. Meeks asked.

"How did you know?"

"Because I'm looking at arteries with troubled blood flow. We call this PAD, or Peripheral Artery Disease. PAD is the narrowing or blockage of the vessels that carry blood—oxygen—from the heart to the legs. It is caused by the buildup of plaque in the arteries. This is called atherosclerosis. If not treated, the circulation can be cut off so much that ... in Stage Four, the legs could get gangrene and ...."

"That sounds delightful," said Jerry. "What can be done?"

"Exercise more, eat less fat, and wear compression stockings."

"I can do that."

The compression stockings made all the difference. The pain went away and Jerry was back at the hangar.

"Patience and perseverance have a magical effect before which difficulties disappear and obstacles vanish."
~John Quincy Adams

Chapter 25

The Alien

The following year, Jerry was suddenly struck with severe pain in his abdomen. Lisa took him to the emergency room. After scans, they were all surprised to discover that the problem was not acute appendicitis. It was a mystery.

The family physician, Dr. Peterson, met with them in the emergency room. "Because of the severity of your pain, I'm admitting you, and will schedule exploratory surgery for tomorrow. I've got a hotshot surgeon, Dr. Williams, who can get in and out with a good look around and a biopsy. He has zero bedside manner, but he's a great tech, and that's what we want."

Once into his hospital room, Jerry received painkillers that took the edge off, but he was clearly suffering. The surgery couldn't come soon enough.

"Lymphoma," said the surgeon, as they wheeled Jerry out of the operating room the next morning. "I think. Let's see how the biopsy comes out."

Jerry continued to be in severe pain. The biopsy returned negative for lymphoma.

"I don't believe it," said the surgeon. "Let me go in and look again and get a bigger piece."

"Could you say that again? I must have misunderstood you," said Lisa.

"I know it's lymphoma. I need to get a bigger piece of it."

Lisa shook her head. Then she looked at Jerry, still groggy from the anesthesia. She closed her eyes and took a deep breath.

Two days later, Dr. Williams operated again. The biopsy returned negative.

"I'm sure it's lymphoma," the surgeon said again.

"Okay. What if it is lymphoma? What's the treatment for lymphoma?" asked Lisa.

"Chemotherapy and radiation."

"Then we'd better get a definitive diagnosis before treating," replied Lisa.

"Yes, you're right," said Dr. Williams. "But I know it's lymphoma. It has to be."

He's a hotshot alright, thought Lisa.

Jerry continued to be in acute pain. Morphine and Fentanyl made a dent but didn't remove it entirely.

Dr. Peterson came into the hospital room the next day. He looked out the window, gave a sigh, and then turned to us. "I don't know what to do. I can't get a diagnosis. I do know that it's a mass in your lower gut that has tentacles attached to your intestines. We can treat for pain, but that's not solving the problem. It's not looking good."

He nodded quietly to Lisa, who followed him out into the hallway. They let the door close. Lisa leaned against the wall and took a deep breath.

Dr. Peterson was grave. "It's not removable. We don't know what it is. It appears to be growing and highly inflamed. I think it could kill him within weeks. If it grows more around the organs, it will squeeze the life out of them."

"I know you're doing everything you can," said Lisa.

"Your last-ditch resort is the University of Miami research center. Let them see if they can get it out," said Dr. Peterson.

They went back into the room. Dr. Peterson laid out the options.

"I'll try anything," said Jerry. "The pain is crazy."

Lisa named it the Alien.

They went to the University of Miami. Jerry was in so much pain that they would walk about fifteen steps and he would stop to get his strength. He was doubled over. Everyone passing by stopped to help and ask if he was okay. They encountered kindness everywhere as strangers observed the difficulties.

After an agonizing wait, they were ushered into the medical office of the best intestinal surgeon in the southeast. Dr. Krisha read through the medical charts, audibly gasping and clucking, and shaking his head from side to side.

"Okay, got it. I can do this. What I will do is pull all your intestines out on to the table and snip off these tendrils." Dr. Krisha waved his arms, pointing to the x-rays and MRI scans on the wall viewers. "It will be a long operation with a long recovery period, and you have a 50 percent chance of dying. But of course, that means you also have a 50 percent chance of living." Dr. Krisha smiled at Jerry. Lisa was quiet.

"When you say a long recovery period, what exactly does that mean?" asked Jerry.

"Four months. Three surgeries."

"Never mind," said Jerry.

They returned to Dr. Peterson to report on the alternatives.

"I have another idea," Dr. Peterson said. "I agree that a 50 percent success rate is not tenable. I have a contact at the Mayo Clinic in Rochester, Minnesota. Are you willing to go there for a consult?"

"Yes," said Jerry. "Whatever we need to do."

They flew to the Mayo Clinic. They were there for three days for tests and labs. Under different circumstances, it would have been a fun trip. The warren of underground passages, shops, and restaurants was something they'd never seen. The medical complex was large and interesting.

They received even more attention as Jerry stopped to catch his breath in the hallways, doubled over in pain. He had medication for the pain, but it didn't quite take the ache away. People would stop and ask if they could do anything.

"This is embarrassing," said Jerry.

"People want to help," replied Lisa. "The kindness of strangers lives on."

They arrived at Dr. Baker's office and were ushered straight in. Dr. Baker, a tall man in his thirties, greeted them with a smile.

"This is the oddest thing I have ever seen," said Dr. Baker. "No, it is not lymphoma, and it's not a cancer. I suspect it may be a late response to the cobalt radiation you got when you were younger. Have you been exposed to any toxic chemicals over time, say, enamels or paints?"

"Like spraying paint on an airplane without a mask?" said Jerry sheepishly.

"Exactly like that, yes. But perhaps not. I can't tell you for sure, but it's probably a combination of exposures. Or, like some cancers, it could simply be happenstance. What you have is called Mesenteric Enteritis. It is impossible to get out without removing portions of your small and large intestines; there are too many attachments, and that is why you are in so much pain. I'm going to devise a drug regimen for you I am hoping will reduce the mass and the inflammation."

"Have you seen this before, Dr. Baker?" asked Lisa.

"Yes. But only a few cases, and not in the United States. It's extremely rare."

"That's Jerry," said Lisa.

Jerry began the drug chemotherapy immediately. After four weeks, the pain was gone, and he was back at work.

For the Love of an Airplane

"It's not the strength of the body that counts, but the strength of the spirit."
~J.R.R. Tolkien

Chapter 26

Incidental Findings

One day in 2012, Jerry was building a wing for a Stearman. He felt some tingling in his right hand. It was odd; it wasn't as if the hand had gone to sleep, but he had trouble moving it. One of the employees, Adam, was in the workshop with him, working on an avionics panel.

"Hmm," said Jerry.

Adam looked up. "What?"

Jerry thought of what he wanted to say, that he was feeling strange, but no words would come out. "Ah ...." He shook his head and pointed to his hand by his side.

Adam dialed 911 and then called Lisa. "Stroke, I think," he said.

Lisa reached the emergency room at exactly the same time the ambulance did. Lisa followed the gurney in as the medics shouted, "Stroke!" They began treatment immediately. Lisa filled the staff in on all the medical history.

Jerry was in the hospital for four days. He was lucky; he'd had a TIA, or Transient Ischemic Attack, and recovered quickly. A consequence of the testing also revealed an aneurysm in the front section of his brain. The doctors were sure that it wasn't involved in his attack, but they made a referral to a neurologist. When Jerry was feeling better, they drove two hours to Asheville, North Carolina, to Mission Hospital.

Dr. Robbins came into the exam room and pulled up the images on a DICOM viewer.

"As you may know, an aneurysm is a weakened or bulging area in the wall of an artery. If the blood pressure is strong, and the weakness expands, then it can burst. This one is in your brain, right here." He placed his finger at the top of Jerry's forehead. "The good news is that we don't think this was involved in the stroke you had recently."

"What's the bad news?" asked Lisa.

"The bad news is that it could rupture at any time. That's lights out."

"Sort of like having a little piece of dynamite in you that could go off?" said Jerry.

"Sort of, yes."

"Great," said Jerry.

"It could have been there from birth, though. Anyway, I can seal it. It's a surgery where I can go in direct, or with a catheter. It's not without some risk, but it's routine."

"How long to get back to work?" asked Jerry.

"Two weeks."

"What if we don't do anything?" asked Jerry.

"Then we'll watch it for changes."

"That sounds good. We'll watch it."

"That's fine, but there's something else I'd like to do."

"Yes?"

"Did you know you have a severe case of scoliosis?"

"Yes, that's why I can't walk straight and my back hurts when I stand. Are you saying you can fix that?"

"I can't, but my colleague, an orthopedic surgeon, can. I'll refer you. In any case, I want you back here in four months to look at the aneurysm. That can take you out in a heartbeat. Literally."

Their next specialist appointment was with the orthopedic surgeon. He looked with glee at the musculoskeletal rendering on the scans and x-rays in front of him.

"I can fix this!" he said to Jerry, like a carpenter waving a hammer at a nail. It sounded familiar.

Jerry looked at the scans. "Goodness gracious, the bones are all bent up and bent over. No wonder I have trouble walking."

"That's what I'm saying. I'm not sure why you're not in a wheelchair."

"No one told that to the skeleton," said Jerry. "Okay, tell me what's involved."

"A complex series of surgeries. We'll start with the hip area, then the spine, then the neck."

"How soon would I be able to get back to work?"

"Get back to work? Probably two years."

"Never mind."

For the Love of an Airplane

Four months later, Jerry returned dutifully to the neurosurgeon.

"The aneurysm looks stable," said the neurosurgeon. "But realize that this could let loose any time. Are you ready for me to fix it?"

"You said I'd be out of work for two weeks?"

"I did."

"Let's keep watching it."

"Okay, come back in six months and let me look at it again. If it gets bigger, I'm going to try to change your mind."

"Okay. Let's see how things go," said Jerry.

"All you need is the plan, the road map, and the courage to press on to your destination."
~Earl Nightingale

Chapter 27

More Lives than a Cat

A year later, Jerry and Lisa were in Florida visiting family and friends. They left to return home from Boynton Beach via Route 75 up the center of the state. Just south of Ocala, Jerry got off at the exit. "Gas?" asked Lisa. "Hmm," uttered Jerry. Lisa thought nothing of it until Jerry pulled into the gas station, turned the truck off, and mumbled, pointing to his right arm, which was limp at his side.

Lisa realized he was back in stroke territory. She ran into the station and dialed 911 from the station phone, knowing it would be located and send an ambulance faster than using the cell phone. It just so happened that a fire rescue truck was passing the station at the same time. Lisa watched the truck turn around in front of them and pull in.

"Stroke."

They started an IV and blood thinners on the spot, and then Lisa followed the truck to the Ocala hospital. Jerry was there a week. This stroke was a more serious version of the TIAs he'd had earlier. Lisa spent the days in the room with Jerry, and the staff came to love his sense of humor. They'd come in sometimes just to talk airplanes.

When they finally got home the following week, Jerry asked to go straight to the hangar. When they arrived there, his guys cheered for him as he got out of the truck. Then the jokes started. Jerry was feeling better already.

"Look, they get more done when I'm gone than when I'm here," said Jerry.

"You should rest at home," said Lisa.

"I can rest at the hangar." They both laughed. Jerry was definitely in recovery.

A follow-up with the cardiologist brought blood thinners and blood pressure drugs into the pharmacological cocktail every day, and it did wonders. After the Florida episode, the ministrokes stopped.

"Your family history of heart disease doesn't help," Lisa said one day. "Every one of your siblings has had either stents or bypass."

"You're right. My whole family had heart disease. Without modern medicine, I wouldn't be here now. In fact, thinking about it, every medical encounter I've had in my life has been filled with compassionate and competent practitioners. I'm fortunate and appreciative. I'll take the great technician any day, but I've been delighted to get good tech combined with friendly bedside manner; I couldn't ask for better."

Eight years later, in 2024, Jerry's urologist went on a hunt to find the source of some internal bleeding found on a routine checkup. After several exploratory surgeries, Jerry was diagnosed with kidney cancer.

"I'd like to yank it out," said the doctor, looking at Jerry. "But at 88 years old, it might not be a good plan for you. Let's get a second opinion."

Specialists agreed that the right kidney should be removed.

Jerry asked the surgeon, "How soon can I return to work?"

The surgeon laughed. "A couple weeks? How long do you want to be out of work?"

"A day?"

The surgeon and the assistants were all laughing.

Lisa said, "He's not kidding."

The surgery was performed that evening, and Jerry returned to the hangar the next afternoon.

For the Love of an Airplane

Part Three: The Stadtmiller Guide to Business

Note to the Reader
2024

When Jerry gives tours of his shop, he gets lots of questions about how he came to open his business, and what his challenges have been. Beginning in 2004, I started keeping notes and began oral history style interviews with Jerry. The following interview is condensed and edited from about 25 hours of audio recordings.

An observation those around Jerry make is, "All the stuff in that brain of yours needs to be downloaded and shared."

Since modern technology can't quite do that yet, I decided the next best thing would be to ask Jerry himself to explain his life and business philosophy. Here it is, in his own words.

For reading simplicity, I will not use double quote marks for dialogue unless someone other than Jerry or the interviewer is speaking. Also for simplicity, I have placed the interview questions in italics.

"The best way to predict the future is to create it."
~Peter Drucker

Chapter 28

Vision for BIPE

What was your vision when you started BIPE?

My vision was, and still is, to invite customers to imagine the airplane they want to own and fly, and as long as it is an antique fabric covered aircraft, I would do it for them. Tube and fabric is my specialty. I'd rather have that be my calling card than to do everything for everybody.

They could fly in something they just wanted covered, they could fly in something they wanted restored, they could bring me junk on a trailer. If that's what they wanted, I would figure it out. Sometimes I'd help them by looking for a basket case or a project in pieces.

The key is that the customer decides exactly what they want; I don't decide what they want. I can compare it to house building; you can build a nice house and hope someone likes it and buys it, or you can find out exactly what the customer wants and build it.

They have to agree to the terms. They buy the airplane and parts, I will restore it. I can't afford to go out and buy a variety of projects and then rebuild them, hoping to sell to the right person. Not only would that be expensive, it might not be what the customer wants.

Many of my customers bring me an airplane that they have had in the family for generations. When they come to visit the project and especially when it's complete and they come to test fly it, they get very emotional.

Last week I had a customer come to make his first test flight in his PA-18 Super Cub. Here's the letter I got from him.

"Jerry, please put this tribute on your website. I want everyone to know how amazing this experience has been."

> When it came to restoring a beloved 1950 Piper Super Cub passed down from my father, I was intent on ensuring such an important job ended up in the right hands. I searched here in the United States for a restoration shop I could trust. Interactions with a number of specialists across the country left me disappointed. Then I came across BIPE. Meeting Jerry and his team, visiting the shop, and speaking with past clients convinced me I had found what I was looking for: an experienced, high integrity operation that would treat my aircraft as though it were their own, with the same pride and an unwavering commitment to quality, care, and attention to detail as I would

lavish on it. Of course, there were twists and turns along the journey, as there always will be with a project of this magnitude, but Jerry was transparent, fair, and—above all—a trusted partner from start to finish. I am beyond thrilled with the result, and deeply grateful to BIPE for resurrecting N7106K, a family heirloom, and restoring her to stunning new flying condition."

—Patrick Clark, August 30th, 2024

I'm not trying to toot my own horn as much as demonstrate how this passion and love for aircraft drives the life of my business. A letter like that from a customer means the world to me. It's why I do what I do. Sometimes customers send me pictures of the awards they win with the airplane. Same thing; it pleases me so much.

Years ago, I began taking color photographs of the customer airplanes when they left to go home. I put a description with each one and hung it on the wall. I've run out of wall space.

When you started out, it was just you?

Yes. That way, I had complete control over the work. I wished I could find some good helpers, but at the time, I was too concerned about how the work was done. It took years before I realized I could train others to do what I was doing. I knew nothing about how to train someone. Coincidentally, about that time, I got a call from a good friend, Ron Alexander. This was in the 1990s.

For the Love of an Airplane

"Jerry, I need you to teach fabric covering for me."

"Teach? Ron, I don't know how to teach."

"But you know fabric inside out; I can teach you how to teach."

Ron Alexander owned SportAir, a collection of workshops designed to help people build their own airplanes. Because Ron also owned Alexander Airplane Company, I bought supplies from him. We both shared a passion for building and flying vintage aircraft.

Ron asked me to meet with him. He explained the workshops. While I wasn't comfortable standing in a classroom learning or teaching anything else, fabric covering was easy, since I loved it so much. My fear of speaking melted away, just as Ron said it would.

After several years of teaching the workshops, I could get in front of a group of people and feel comfortable, even happy to be there. I was so surprised! After that, I started volunteering at aviation shows like Sun-N-Fun and Oshkosh. I continued teaching the SportAir classes after the EAA (Experimental Aircraft Association) took it over. It was a breakthrough for me.

Lisa Turner

So, you could teach helpers?

Yes. Usually, you can tell right away if someone has the drive and the aptitude for the fabric covering work, which is what our business is built around. Within a short time, I can determine if someone has the expertise and enjoyment for it. The details are critical. They have to get it right every time they tie a knot or do an inspection as they disassemble parts.

Having a few part-time helpers was a big factor in being able to take on a little more work than I could do all by myself, but I still wasn't ready for full-time employees. That came later.

"Proper business planning demands that you focus on the self-interest of the customer at all times."
~Brian Tracy

Chapter 29

Practicalities

What formal training did you get in business?

None. About the only thing that helped me was my shop teacher, who said I'd be good at aviation, and my National Guard instructor, who taught me discipline and ethics.

How long were you in the National Guard?

Three years. It was a good experience even though the military was not a favorite thing for me; but since I got to work on aircraft and avionics, I was happy. I had no desire to see combat.

What advice did your National Guard instructor offer you?

He said that the way you treat customers defines a business. You can insult them, you can insult their friends, you can swear at them, but if you cheat them out of one single cent, they will abandon you. Honesty and integrity are at the core of the relationship.

What was your biggest challenge starting out?

At first, I envisioned a business where I could train and manage many employees to turn out top-notch restorations. I noticed early that there was a direct relationship between how good the work was and how many trainees I had. It takes a while for people to learn the work, along with the secrets and details. If I was heavily involved, the work went faster and there were fewer mistakes.

I realized the business had to be balanced between work output and money coming in. More work means more money, but if the quality is not there, then the business isn't working right. Every time I got a little bigger, with more airplanes, I'd realize that I wasn't sticking to my vision for what I wanted for my customers. It's a matter of scale and balance; like a teeter-totter.

The lesson I learned from this is that the price point and the workload output have to match. I have to have enough work to get paid, but not so much that I am not intimately involved in the work production. Over time, I've had a few craftspeople who stuck with me and could easily open their own fabric covering shop, and did. But most of the time it's tough to hold on to an employee long term. Their situation changes, or they tire of the work, or medical circumstances intervene.

Right now, we have five airplanes underway. I'd say we are maxed out at the level required to get the work done with the highest level of quality. Taking on more employees is not the answer.

Who runs the office?

I do. I do the parts ordering, the customer invoices and letters, the phone calls, the emails, the FAA paperwork, and the accounting. Although I'm comfortable with email, Lisa keeps the accounting up to date and runs the website. Lisa tells me I didn't get the computer "tech-gene," and I know she's right.

What does a typical work day look like for you?

I check in with the guys first to make sure they are working on the right things. I answer questions and may provide a little help with a process. Then I hit the computer. Email and customer communications come first. I return phone calls. Then parts ordering and accounting. Finally, I write up invoices and work accomplished on draw schedules. Then back to check in with the guys.

Each employee has a detailed work log that they fill out. This way I know how much time the job took, and what customer gets charged for what labor. I flat rate the labor, because otherwise it can get out of hand. When I write up the invoicing, I tell the customer exactly where every hour of labor went.

"It takes 20 years to build a reputation and five minutes to ruin it."
~Warren Buffett

Chapter 30

Ethics

How would you describe the core values of your business?

Our business philosophy is distinct. Integrity and safety weave through the relationships with our customers. Money does not come first. We don't ask for deposits or up-front payments.

We will try to under-commit and over-deliver. We hold the customer's vision of what they want constant as we work on their project. We'll try to save the customer money everywhere we can, but will never, ever, sacrifice safety or quality to do so.

Ethics is at the core of the business. Let me tell you a story. We had a customer, Ed, who we restored multiple airplanes for. He himself was an amazing businessman. He appreciated how we ran BIPE. Several years after we completed his last restoration, he came into the shop. He enjoys coming by and checking on

For the Love of an Airplane

what we're working on and chatting. I invited Ed to take a seat in the workroom, where I was working on an avionics panel.

"Jerry, I want to tell you what happened last month. Because of how you do business, you'll appreciate this. I had my red Stearman for sale. A guy here on the airport, Bret, asked if I could come down on the price. I said, 'Sure.' I told him I'd give him $3K off. We shook hands.

Several days later, he called me and said that $3K was not enough of a discount. I said, 'We shook on the deal, Bret.'

'I know we did. But I need $5K off.'

'We shook on the deal,' I said to Bret again.

'Okay then, forget the $5K,' said Bret. 'We can go back to the $3K discount.'

'The airplane sells for $175K if you still want it,' I said to Bret. I was starting to get annoyed.

'Oh no! That's the original price!' Bret said to me. 'Okay, okay, I'll take it at the $3K off, at $172K, like we first agreed.'

'Nope. Airplane's no longer for sale,' I said back to Bret. Now I was really annoyed.

'What? Okay, $175K,' said Bret.

Now I'd had it. I said, 'Nope. Airplane's not for sale.'

'No, wait, come on Ed, I said I'd pay the full asking of $175K.'

'Nope. Airplane's no longer for sale.'

'Okay, okay, look, you have to sell me the airplane. I'll give you $178K for it,' said Bret.

'Nope. Airplane's not for sale. Thanks, Bret. Goodbye.'

That was it. I was not going to sell my airplane to that guy. He just didn't get it. We made a deal, and we shook hands. Then he reneges.

A week later, he called again. I said no. After another few weeks, I finally put it back on the market after Bret bought something else. It's about principles. It's about fair dealing. It's not about money."

I love that story; it says it all.

Another example I'll give you is being faithful to the safety of the people who are going to get into any airplane that you work on. Being thorough and legal are paramount.

If I'm asked to do an annual inspection on an airplane, I look at every nook and cranny, find every fault I can, follow every regulation I can, and honor the detail that needs to be in the logbooks. There's something in this business called "pencil whipping," and you can imagine what that is. It's not digging deep to really get the airplane as safe as possible.

I've had owners ask me to perform an annual inspection and then get mad at me because I found lots of problems that needed to be fixed. They say, "Gee, when Tom did the annual last year, he didn't find all that stuff." No, he didn't find all that stuff because he didn't look. He decided that, because the airplane was flying, everything was okay. That's dangerous. I don't care how mad an owner gets at me, I'm going to look at every single thing. I routinely find items that were flagged in service bulletins or

For the Love of an Airplane

ADs that were never accomplished in the first place. (Interviewer's note: an AD, or Airworthiness Directive, is issued by the FAA to correct an unsafe condition.)

I've gotten to the point where the only annual I will do now is on the airplanes that we rebuild, because I know what's there.

"You don't run out of time; you run out of attention."
~Lisa Turner

Chapter 31

Time Management

How do you manage your time? How do you get things done?

I list out what needs to be done on each airplane in the form of a draw schedule. I list out the time and the cost, plus what parts I will need. Then I start on it.

Here's the key to the system: I cannot commit to a completion date for the customer. I have to leave it open-ended. I explain this in great detail to a prospective customer. If they are uncomfortable with their project being open-ended, I suggest they go somewhere else. There are too many unknowns, puzzles, and surprises during a restoration. I've taken apart airplanes that flew in with hidden subsurface issues such as cracked spars and corroded structure, sight unseen under the fabric. "Gee, it flew fine," says the customer. It turns out that he or she is lucky something didn't break loose on the way here.

For the Love of an Airplane

When the customer brings me the airplane, we spend time together going over the draw schedule and the timeline, reminding them that there is no way to predict when the airplane will be finished. I have found that the draw schedule and the open-ended finish date make the customer much more comfortable with the timeline, even when they don't know when they can fly it home. The amount of detail they get builds trust in the schedule. It's not like handing someone your credit card and wondering when or if you'll get it back.

How do you manage your own time? What if you don't get everything done on your to-do list?

I don't worry about it. I'm sure that sounds irresponsible, but it works. The list of things to do is never-ending. It's stressful to make a list and not get it all done. While I do have the schedule for the airplane, I don't fret over the day-to-day happenings. That saves energy for the things that matter.

So you don't use a time management system of some sort?

No. The guys have a whiteboard in the shop, and they list out what needs to be done and when. They know better than I do what the timing is because they're working on the projects. They have excellent suggestions for timing when, for example, several airplanes need paint, but we only have one paint booth. They also know better than I do how to move the parts and pieces around the shop to fit the workspaces.

That's unusual, you know; most people stress a lot over deliverables.

To me, that's not logical. There are things you can't do anything about. Why stress out about them? It's unnecessary. Concentrate on the things you have control over, realizing that those things are also going to be variable.

Sort of zen-like.

It's logic. As humans, we have a see-saw relationship with emotion. It's emotion that ends up causing trouble. I'm not saying that emotion isn't a delightful and wonderful thing; just that it's not controllable. I've had customers who were so intent on getting a certain airplane project that they were unable to see the faults in the aircraft. Some of these customers wouldn't listen to reason, and they spent a lot more money and time than they thought they would. I try to bring perspective to the relationship, but sometimes I can't influence them. And I avoid saying "I told you so," later. Just chalk it up to runaway passion. Not much we can do about that. It's happened to me.

I warn customers that there will be emotional moments in the restoration—surprises—that will upset them. No matter how prepared we are for those moments, we can't control the feelings about it. It's a journey and a process; we sometimes have to wait for the feelings to settle down before making decisions.

When faced with these moments, I try to be a good listener for the customer because letting them express themselves helps us move past the event. An example is making the assumption that the airplane that flew in just fine is not going to have cracks in the spar. We find hidden damage all the time, and it adds a new level of complexity, and cost, to the restoration.

The other upsetting thing is when the customer purchases a "basket case,"—which is what we call an airplane in boxes—and assumes that all the parts and pieces are there because the seller told them they were. I've never seen an airplane arrive on a trailer that didn't have missing parts.

"There is only one boss. The customer. And he can fire everybody in the company from the chairman on down, simply by spending his money somewhere else.
~Sam Walton

Chapter 32

Customers

What is your process for finding and engaging customers?

Customers arrive here after either talking to people who have had work done here, or researching BIPE and landing on the website. About 20 percent of my work is repeat customers who keep coming back for more restorations or for more covering jobs.

What do you look for in a customer?

He or she has to communicate with me. From what they want, to understanding how the draw schedule is going to work, is critical. When we first talk about schedule and go over the contract,

I tell them we may run into things that will extend the time we have the airplane. Each of these circumstances will require communication and understanding. If they can agree on those things and will work with us and be patient, they will be a great customer.

What is your process for a restoration?

I have multiple highly defined stages. The first is the customer interview. They are assessing me and I'm assessing them. Can we communicate? Can we trust each other? Is the customer willing to accept my timeline? I ask lots of questions. If I think the customer is not serious, or is not willing to work with me through the process, then I will discourage them. If I think they will work with me, and it appears to be a fit, then I'll encourage them.

The next stage is the contract. I go over the contract with the customer, and I explain the draw schedule and how that will roll out to them.

What percentage does the customer put down in deposit?

Nothing. I don't take any money up front. Why? I haven't produced any work. I don't charge until I've made progress and finished something on the schedule.

Go on.

Next is the disassembly. It is critical that the airplane be inspected thoroughly before anything happens on rebuilding. We make extensive notes on condition, listing questions we need information on. This includes what is missing as well as what we have. We take lots of pictures. We make sure the registration matches the data tag. We label and inventory contents. If the airplane is in boxes and pieces, we inventory everything and make notes about things we have questions about.

Damaged Wing

After disassembly and inventory, we do a close-up and thorough inspection of absolutely everything. We find the tiniest of cracks in wood spars that could create a failure in the future over time, or the beginnings of internal corrosion on a tube that could

For the Love of an Airplane

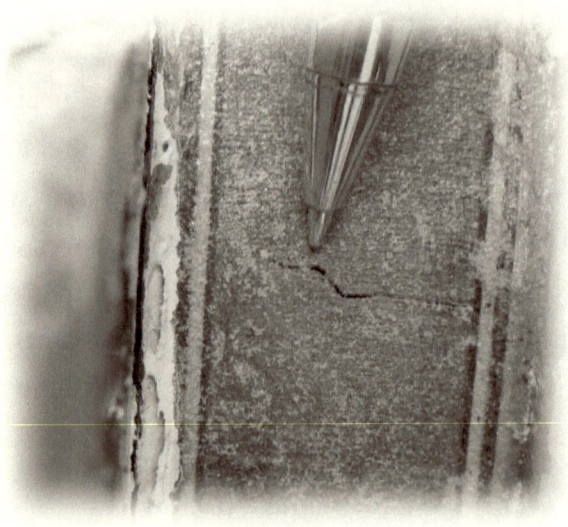

Hidden crack

create a structural failure in flight. We find dead mice, nests, toys, and other strange objects inside wings and fuselages. We use a magnifier and take a lot of time looking at materials and moving things. It's so important to find and fix these well before the airplane is reassembled and covered. I've seen some airplanes on their second or third re-cover that were never examined closely before cover; some of the cracks and damage have been there for a very long time. It's a tribute to the toughness of the airplane, but worries me every time I find it.

Then we begin on the frame-up rebuild. Everything is cleaned, primed, painted. At this stage, we also can find cracks, voids, or damage. I communicate progress to the customer and reaffirm the draw schedule with them. I take photographs. I also go over any extra costs associated with the surprises or damage we find.

Wasps and Mice

The engine gets shipped to the overhaul shop if that was on the list of to-dos.

As we do the work, the draw schedules roll out, and we invoice the customer with a detailed listing of what has been spent down to the penny. We photograph the progress and print out large color photos that we place inside the invoice package, along with a personal detailed letter from me covering progress.

As we go, I do the FAA paperwork in preparation for the logbook updates. This takes a lot of time. On a certified aircraft, the FAA requires documentation of work accomplished, as well as approvals for other things the customer may want—like smoke systems, a better set of brakes, metal fuel tank covers, adding electrical, and other customizations. Without the approvals and documentation, the airplane is not legal to fly. If we need a DER (Designated Engineering Representative) then that adds another layer of complexity as well as cost and management time.

One area I find delightful is helping the customer determine a paint scheme. They can have whatever they want. Do they just want a nice paint job of their choice, or do they want historical accuracy? I show them examples in the books I have.

As we near the end on a restoration, we have lots of details to attend to. Then the aircraft must be flight tested. Sometimes the customer does the testing if they are current in the airplane, and if they're feeling a little rusty, we can locate an experienced pilot for them.

Then we do the fine tuning and address any nits we see. Typically, the rigging is so good that we don't need to make a lot of adjustments.

Then we have a customer for life. I've got several customers who keep coming back with airplanes to work on.

Are there any shortcuts you discovered?

Yes. Not skipping any steps!

"Everything is hard before it is easy."
~Goethe

Chapter 33

Employees

How do you know what you need in the way of help day to day?

It's a dance when it comes to help. When people come to the shop looking for work, they are usually looking for money. This business is not one where people can walk in and do the job straightaway. They have to be trained. In fact, people who say they have done fabric covering before usually have taken on bad habits that I have to spend time breaking.

I'll have A&Ps (Airframe and Powerplant mechanics) show up looking for a job here and say they were earning an enormous salary in some metro area. I am as polite as I can be when I tell them what I can afford to pay. They fall off the chair and say thank you and leave. If I find someone who understands that this work is a journey, and if they love doing it and are willing to learn it, then it will offer a future of enjoyment and possibly a decent

For the Love of an Airplane

living. The love of the work has to come before the money. Many of my past employees will tell you it was worth it, and now they are making a good living at it. When I left Florida to move the business to North Carolina, one of the employees there decided to open their own fabric covering business. He's been in business fifteen years now and loves it.

I see on the website that you accept apprentices?

There was a time when things were so busy in Florida I needed more full-timers. I offered to train them in trade for a very low wage, with the promise that pay would go up as they learned. It's a great system, but no one can afford to work for almost nothing. It used to be that to become a pilot, you'd have to invest a lot of money and time in training yourself and wait for the salary when you were accepted into a major airline. It's not as tough now, but it's along the same principles. Kids go to college and pay for their education; while the learning curve here isn't four years, it's probably at least one year for the basics. When I'm training someone, my other employees are often involved. So, it's pretty expensive for me to train someone. I'm always hoping that when I do, they will stay with me.

Speaking of passion, I have also had people show up here who wanted to work for nothing. They just really enjoy the work.

Lisa Turner

How do you find good employees?

I've never figured that out. I don't want to advertise the position because the pay is so low. Before it's a crisis, someone usually walks in asking for a job. I can tell in the first few weeks if there's a fit. My other guys can tell me right away. I always look for honesty and reliability first, because I can train someone. The third thing is the willingness and ability to learn. Not everyone has that. Finally, if they enjoy what they are doing, then they are likely to stay.

What do you look for in an employee?

Honesty, integrity, reliability, and trainability. I need people who understand that making mistakes is a normal and natural part of the work. I've had a few people who got so upset they made a mistake they let that interfere with the job. We all make mistakes; what's important is to recognize it, admit, correct it, and move on. If someone tries to hide a mistake, I'll fire them on the spot. We can't have that.

How do you recognize talent?

It's more about will than talent. Someone can be very talented, but not do anything with it. You cannot change someone. I dislike when someone says, "If only they would ...." If someone doesn't like something, they are not going to suddenly like it. Accept what the person gives you, and recognize what they want to do, not what they should do. I believe that works across all relationships.

What's your leadership style?

Communication, communication, communication. Everyone working here understands what I expect, and will get feedback, good and bad. Employees know I trust them, or they wouldn't be here.

If an employee is uncomfortable getting unpleasant feedback, they won't last long here. I tell them it's not them I am complaining about; it's what they are doing. I remind them we all make mistakes, and all I want is for them to own up to them and know how to correct what they did.

Before an employee works here, I tell them I'm going to communicate a lot, and expect them to tell me how things are going and be honest. Then I tell them I'm not going to stand over their shoulder and watch unless they want me to at the beginning. They will get the job done without me harping at them. But I expect them to ask me for help when they need it.

How do you handle discipline when an employee doesn't show up for work or isn't honest?

We have a manual that covers schedule, policies, benefits, and safety, so there's no excuse for not knowing. But the key to performance is communication. If people don't know what's expected, they can't perform.

What would your employees say about your management style?

I'm demanding, but I have a good sense of humor. They know they can talk to me anytime. They don't have to wait for me to "be in a good mood," before telling me something they screwed up on. I don't hold grudges, and I don't favor one employee over the other. I don't put up with talking behind another employee's back. I expect and reward honesty.

Have you had any women work for you?

Yes, I have. Quite a few, actually. And very competent and reliable women. Once I explain what I need, and tell them my philosophy on communication and training, they get it right away. I have had a few women work for me long term that were the hardest working employees I've had here. I would love to see more women go into the business.

How do you advertise your business? What marketing do you do?

I've never advertised the business. I keep a list of customers wanting to bring their airplane in; why advertise? Many times I've looked at the list as it has dwindled down to a few airplanes—meaning that work would dry up in two years—but then in the space of those two years, the list re-expands, and I realize that I'm worried for no good reason.

Lisa suggested starting a website for BIPE, so that we could advertise aircraft for sale and to attract employees. Since she could set it up and maintain it, I said fine. The cost is minimal, and customers can even watch the work being done in the shop through the cams we have in the workrooms. I don't pretend to understand any of the computer side of it, but I do know that it's great for my customers. We've loaded lots of video on the site. There are two ways to get to it—Restoreyourairplane.com and Bipeinc.com.

I'll look ahead in the schedule, and see that in 18 months we will have finished everything in the shop. I start worrying. The next day someone calls with a project. I don't pretend to understand it, but somehow good fortune follows me around and I always have a waiting list of airplanes to come in.

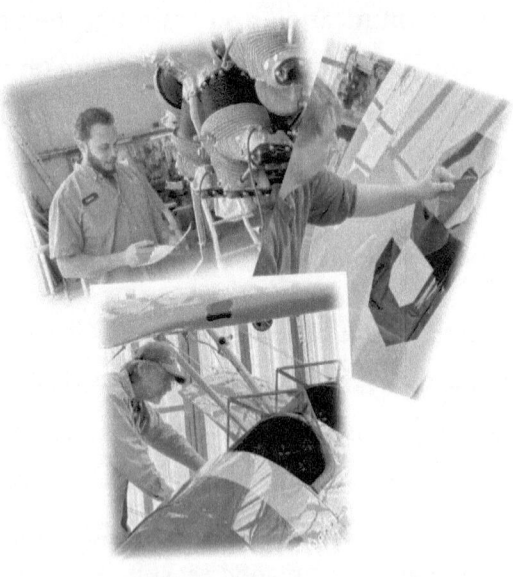

"Successful design is not the achievement of perfection but the minimization and accommodation of imperfection."
~Henry Petroski

Chapter 34

Trivia

What other services do you offer? On the website, I see pre-purchase inspections, insurance estimates, and free advice. And tours?

First, I want people to get out to the airport. Airports are exciting places. You can see airplanes, get rides, get lessons, and learn about the history of aircraft and how the old machines go together. I give the shop tours for that reason. I love giving the tours. People come here expecting some boring lecture about this airplane and that airplane, not realizing that it can be fun for everyone. I show people how the wooden wings are hand built, the spruce and mahogany used in the interior, and the fabric that is placed on the airplanes. I give demonstrations and answer questions. I love it, especially when a school class comes through and the girls are as excited as the boys.

For the Love of an Airplane

Class Tour of BIPE

I joke with people when they come here for a tour. I tell them the tour costs $8. They think I'm serious. Then they look at me as I'm laughing and realize I'm joking. Of course I don't charge for the tour. I love giving the tour and explaining how we do business. If they bring their kids, we put the child in one of the cockpits and they take a picture. That will be a nice keepsake for the future—their child in a 1930s or 1940s era aircraft. Schools and youth groups come out for the tour. It may be the only time the kids get to see a piece of history like this.

The $8 tour joke is so much fun, I've had people mail me $8 in play money, and once a thank you note arrived with eight one-dollar bills in it.

It's unfortunate that airports are now closed off to the public. It's hard to get to see everything because they've put up fences and gates. People think we don't want them interrupting our day, or we're working on dangerous things. We're just having fun all day, and we'd like to share that.

The extra services have to do with the aviation community in general. When someone needs information and advice, I am happy to help. I never charge anyone for this advice over the phone or email. If I do a pre-buy, I warn the customer that I'm going to be thorough and find things that upset them, and I do charge for that. But if I find one thing that is not right or is a risk, I flag it, and it's worth the price to the prospective owner.

I see movie sets on the website? What is that about?

I've had filmmakers call me to see if they can use the airplanes in a backdrop or documentary. Whatever we can do, I'm ready for it. I also have museums and historians call to make sure their facts are straight on the airplanes. The Discovery channel called once to verify an aircraft model they were using in a documentary. It's not a good thing when commentators and screenwriters get the facts wrong on history. I love listening to World War II documentaries on audio, but I find they routinely get things wrong on the technical details.

For the Love of an Airplane

I try to be careful with my friends though, because I can get obnoxious. One time I attended a get-together of homebuilt aircraft owners with Lisa. They're a wonderful bunch of builders and pilots, and they are as excited and interested in the history of aviation and the old airplanes as any group I know. The leader of the group decided that an aviation trivia game after dinner would be fun. He started asking the questions, and I kept jumping in, answering them. I didn't realize how annoying I had become, because the rest of the people couldn't get a single word in. Finally, the presenter shouted for me to be quiet.

"Let someone else answer!" said Greg.

I realized that in my excitement, I had literally taken over the party.

As I sat there, minding my own business, I saw Greg give the wrong answer to an identification question. I started to speak up, then got quiet again as the guys looked at me sternly.

Later, I met up with Greg to apologize but also to tell him that several slides were wrong. He was friendly and told me he appreciated my help. We sat down and went through the slides and got them all corrected.

Another time, I was on an aviation museum tour. The tour guide was giving the wrong information on the antique and military airplanes. At first I spoke up, but then the guide got upset, so I was quiet. Very disappointing. I just assumed that the guides would know what was there in the museum inside out—like year manufactured, engine type and horsepower, fuel burn, number of passengers, original markings, and so forth.

One time I was visiting with Lisa's family in Northeast Harbor, Maine. When we drove on to the island, I noticed a sightseeing business with biplanes. I was outside early one day when one of the airplanes flew over. I noticed the Waco was red and white. That afternoon, we were inside in the living room with the windows open. We heard the biplane flying over.

"Jerry, what airplane keeps flying over the house?" asked Lisa's brother Jeffrey.

"A Waco YMF-5 with a 300 horsepower Jacobs R755A2, 7-cylinder radial engine."

Jeffrey was startled. "Okay, Smarty-Pants, what color is the airplane?"

Jerry paused a moment, shutting his eyes with his head tilted up. "Red with white stripes."

"What? How can you figure the color from hearing it? Let me look." Jeff went outside and looked up. Red. He came back in, shaking his head.

"How in the world did you know that?"

"The engine is the heart of the airplane, but the pilot is its soul."
~Walter Raleigh

Chapter 35

Lessons

Many of the stories when you were growing up had some kind of lesson in it. Have those experiences helped you?

Yes. Take the early days when I collected bricks from an old building nearby that had collapsed. I pulled the bricks out and put them in my cart and dragged them home. I started out thinking I would just play with them, but then I got the idea to build a fire pit that was actually usable. When the neighbor saw it, she asked if I could build one for her. I said, "Sure." She gave me seventy-five cents. I saved the money. Then other neighbors saw her fire pit. They came to me to build one for them. The work kept on coming. So now I save money instead of spending it.

For the Love of an Airplane

Another is when I had cancer and the guys at Riley Aeronautics came behind me to fix what I screwed up. It's so important to check, check, check. Airplanes can kill people. Everything has got to be right. If I have a trainee that doesn't like the rest of us checking his or her work, they can't stay with me. We all check each other's work.

Then of course there's the five Wacos story. I realized that you have to communicate with people, even when you don't want to, and that investing in something now may give you a good return later. If I had called that guy, I would have had at least several airplanes I could rebuild, if not all five. Imagine that! I could still kick myself for not calling that guy.

How is the business different now than it was when you began it?

The amount of work and the efficiencies we've built in. Right now, I have a five-year waiting list. But the size is right where it should be.

What do you think differentiates you from other repair or restoration shops?

Not asking for money up front and the level of customer communication. The full report with photographs that we put in with the invoices. The personal letter that I write to the customer with every single invoice. The photographs we put on a USB drive for the customer. The cameras that we have on in the shop workspaces 24 hours a day.

Speaking of the cameras, we have one customer now who watches the work on his airplane for hours. If we move the airplane around to make room for another one, or move it for cleaning, he calls and asks me what did we do with his airplane?

What is your biggest challenge now?

Finding people able to afford to come here and be trained. They have to be trainable; they have to be reliable; they have to be honest, and they have to commit to a long-term relationship. It's tough spending the time and energy to train someone and then lose them after four or six months. The draw has to be the joy of working on antique aircraft, knowing that they are making a difference.

Once a trainee is really up to speed, what they earn goes up quite a bit. But the quality and the competence have to be there.

What upsets you now in the course of business?

Finding out we made a mistake. Things have to be top-notch. If we discover something we missed, it has to be done over. We lose a lot of money on re-doing things, but thankfully it's rare. If we make a mistake, I let the customer know immediately so they understand what we're doing.

The other thing that upsets me is if we have a customer that is not pleased with something. It can be anything. If they are not happy, we will move heaven and earth to correct it to their satisfaction. I've only had a few instances where I wasn't able to

For the Love of an Airplane

please a customer. One time I had a customer who said the work was too good for him. He asked if we could reduce the level of quality. I said no. We only produce one type of work; high quality. That was very bizarre.

I also dislike how the costs are continuing to go up, especially on small parts and hardware. It's gotten so expensive that there are many people who want to restore their airplanes but they simply can't afford it. I've held off raising prices at the expense of my salary. I just don't want to raise the prices. I couldn't care less about my own salary, but then my guys don't seem to feel the same way about theirs!

It's a bad day when the company I order paint from mixes up the slightly wrong color. But we all make mistakes. Or I might give them the wrong number. One time the color was correct, but the shade was wrong. We didn't find out until the airplane got a finish coat of paint. It's an enormous job to stop and go back and sand all over again in preparation for a new coat on an entire surface.

It's a bad day when UPS shows up with a pallet of paint cans with the center cans smashed.

It's a bad day when FedEx shows up with a prop that's just been overhauled that is now damaged in shipment.

It's a bad day when you order a piece of wood trim for the interior of an airplane and the shipping costs more than the trim does.

These things all upset me when they occur, but they are going to happen and you have to move on from it.

Jerry with a 1930 Waco RNF, Pima Air and Space Museum, Tucson, Arizona, 2004

"The only Zen that you find at the top of the mountain is the Zen you bring with you."
~Proverb

Chapter 36

Customer Advice

I'm sure you've seen plenty of errors that customers make, unknowingly, because they don't know where to start when they decide to get their airplane restored. What advice do you have for someone contemplating a restoration?

Yes, some things I've seen are sad to see. I've had many customers end up here after an unpleasant experience elsewhere. There are three big mistakes people make.

The first mistake is writing big checks at the beginning. I've had at least a dozen customers come to me after losing money to someone who might have been well intentioned, but didn't know what they were doing. So the person keeps charging things, and the customer doesn't know what they are for or have any sense of how much the repairs or restoration are going to cost.

I'm not inclined to give business advice to a customer, but I have told some people on consults that there's no good reason to pay up front deposits to a shop unless there is a specific good reason for it. If the business can't support ongoing expenses, I'd be worried.

The second mistake I see is not getting a detailed contract for services. In all the saddest stories about things not going well, this is the big one. Handshakes are fine on direct and simple transactions, but on something like a major repair or a restoration, you want to protect yourself and have a schedule you can count on. All reputable shops have a contract, and they will go over it in detail with the customer.

The third mistake I see is not verifying experience and competence. Whether it's one person working independently, or a shop, you must find out what kind of work they do and how many airplanes they have done that are similar to yours. Do they check airworthiness directives before starting work? Do they check service bulletins? I've seen airplanes that are in for a third or fourth cover job and no one fixed the structure underneath the fabric! This is a recipe for an in-flight failure.

Finally, I always tell people that restorations are full of surprises and to expect them. It's okay; we want to find the tiniest of problems and get them all corrected.

Lisa Turner

What do you think of someone without a mechanic's license who wants to do their own work on their own airplane?

That's fine. They need to study up on the regulations and find an A&P/IA (Airframe and Powerplant with Inspection Authorization) who is willing to oversee their work. I'd tell someone interested in doing this to actually go spend some time as an apprentice at a shop where they can see how things are done.

There are also plenty of excellent workshops the EAA, or Experimental Aircraft Association, put on around the country. For fabric covering skills in particular, I highly recommend attending a hands-on workshop.

"Forget regret, or life is yours to miss."
~Jonathan Larson

Chapter 37

No Regrets

If you had to begin all over again, would you change anything? Do you have any regrets?

I wouldn't change anything. And no regrets. Once I learned from my errors growing up, it helped me see what to watch for now.

What advice would you give to someone starting out in this business?

Don't go into it for the money, go into it for the love of airplanes. Go into it for the happiness of seeing a member of the family get restored to factory fresh flying condition. Go into it for the historical contribution. Go into it to bring joy to the owners. Don't do it unless you love it.

For the Love of an Airplane

Along those lines, what's your vision for the future of BIPE?

My hope is one of my guys or gals takes the business and runs with it. We still have people in this world who can use their knowledge and appreciation of history, along with top craftsmanship and customer service skills to deliver a beautiful and accurate restoration, but the numbers are going down. I would love to see the tradition live on here.

What do you find most difficult in this business now?

The expenses are high. Even though I tell customers we'll definitely have some surprises restoring the airplane, I continue to be surprised myself at some things that hold us up. We can thoroughly leak test a fuel tank, for example, and then it leaks when we have it installed in the airplane. We can get a fully overhauled engine that should run perfectly, not run at all when we begin testing it. Before the test flight, all the gremlins come out of the woodwork. As each gremlin pops up, we have to be thorough in how we banish it.

How do you not stress out?

We don't stress out because we know that it's normal for issues to arise in the course of a total restoration, even a simple cover job, or what we think is a simple repair. It's as if Murphy's Law is laughing at you, but you will get the best of the situation. The key is to accept the surprises and work on each one thoughtfully.

Lisa Turner

Some of the experimental builders have said it the best: "I am 80 percent done and have 80 percent to go."

So if someone wants to replicate what you've done in this business, what is your advice to them?

Realize that the profit point is elusive. If you go into it loving what you are doing, then most of the money problems will self-resolve. This is pricing the job where you can make a living, but the customer is getting a good deal. Watch all the ancillary expenses—the cost of doing business—like taxes and payroll and insurance and rent. Location has a lot to do with this.

Add to that mix integrity in operation, and communication with the customer, and you'll have it made.

So, you've nearly died ten or eleven times already, by my count. You are 88 now. To what do you attribute your longevity?

Perhaps my logical method of thinking which allows me to accept what I have right here and right now with appreciation. I know that sounds canned, but I can't think of anything else that would say it.

When do you plan on retiring?

Retiring? (*laughter*). I'm sure that for people who have "normal" jobs stopping work and then planning out the things you have always wanted to do in life and then doing them is normal. Since I'm already doing what I've always wanted in life, I delight in

For the Love of an Airplane

continuing to do what I adore. I know I can't escape the physics of aging; my hope is that I'll collapse over an airplane wing I'm working on and that will be that. Until then, I can't imagine being any happier than I am right now.

How do you want to be remembered?

I'd like to be remembered as someone who learned from their mistakes in life and adored restoring these vintage airplanes to flying condition. There's nothing that makes me happier than seeing a customer weep in joy as he sees his freshly restored airplane roll out of the hangar. I delight in the contributions I can make to the community of pilots and aircraft owners. All for the love of an airplane.

Lisa Turner

For the Love of an Airplane

Author Note to the Reader

You may wonder why the author hasn't shared the details of Jerry's marriages or the families surrounding them. Jerry himself explains.

"My life is truly defined by airplanes. At home one time a long time ago, I asked if I could spend the weekend at the airport. I was told, 'No. Spend the time with me. I am jealous of your airplanes. They are your mistresses.'

Since that moment, I yearned to be at the airport as I pleased. Of course, anything we perceive we cannot have, we want. But I realized the obligations I had to my relationships in life, and I tried to be a better partner. But this didn't take away the yearning I had for the airport.

Soon after my third marriage, I broached the subject with Lisa. She replied, 'Wonderful! I would love to be at home working on projects myself.' So, I can truly say that I've met my nirvana in all relationships—both with airplanes, customers, and the people I love."

Lisa and Jerry, November 2024 KRHP

Lisa Turner 2024

About the Author

Lisa grew up taking things apart and playing with the boys. After graduating from college with a degree in English, she started a bicycle shop, attended night school for an engineering degree, and took on odd jobs in residential and commercial construction.

Lisa has worked for three major U.S. corporations at the executive level, most notably as Chief Training Officer for Tyco in Boca Raton, Florida. Most recently, Lisa worked as an avionics manufacturing engineer for MOOG in Murphy, North Carolina.

A few of Lisa's avocations are flying and writing. She holds a private pilot license, an FAA (Federal Aviation Administration) airframe and powerplant license (A&P), and she was the first woman to qualify as an AB-DAR, or Amateur-Built Designated

For the Love of an Airplane

Airworthiness Representative for the FAA. Lisa is a member and volunteer for the EAA (Experimental Aircraft Association).

In the 1990s, Lisa built an airplane in her garage—a two-place, 150-mph craft—and flew it from south Florida to Maine and back. Inspired by the experience, she wrote a book about the adventure called *Dream Take Flight*.

Lisa is a columnist for *Sport Aviation* and *KITPLANES* magazines, and writes the weekly home improvement column for the Clay County Progress in her hometown of Hayesville, NC.

For the Love of an Airplane is Lisa's sixth book. From home maintenance advice (*House Keys* and *Home Inspection Answers Guide*), to time management (*Your Simplest Life*), problem-solving (*Team Steps Guide*) and adventure (*Dream Take Flight*), Lisa is always trying to entertain readers.

Lisa's books are available on Amazon, Ingram, and Audible. eBook versions start at $3.99. Go to Lisa's author page or website for more information.

Lisa holds degrees in engineering (A.S.), English (B.A.), business (M.B.A., Ph.D.), and science (Sc.D.).

Author Page: https://www.amazon.com/stores/author/B018O79HFO
Website: https://dreamtakeflight.com/

End Notes

Jerry enjoys this classic song, but would like to change one word in the lyrics.

We'll Meet (Fly) Again

We'll fly again;
Don't know where
Don't know when,
But I know we'll fly again some sunny day.

—Adapted from the *We'll Meet Again* lyrics, composed by Ross Parker and Hughie Charles, and sung by Dame Vera Lynn. First released in 1939

Lisa Turner

NOTES

www.ingramcontent.com/pod-product-compliance
Lightning Source LLC
Chambersburg PA
CBHW020727220426
43209CB00095B/1966/J